Fake News, Propaganda, and Plain Old Lies

Fake News, Propaganda, and Plain Old Lies

How to Find Trustworthy Information in the Digital Age

DONALD A. BARCLAY

ROWMAN & LITTLEFIELD
Lanham • Boulder • New York • London

Published by Rowman & Littlefield
An imprint of The Rowman & Littlefield Publishing Group, Inc.
4501 Forbes Boulevard, Suite 200, Lanham, Maryland 20706
www.rowman.com

Unit A, Whitacre Mews, 26-34 Stannary Street, London SE11 4AB

British Library Cataloguing in Publication Information Available

Library of Congress Cataloging-in-Publication Data

Names: Barclay, Donald A. author.
Title: Fake news, propaganda, and plain old lies : how to find trustworthy
   information in the digital age / Donald A. Barclay.
Description: Lanham : Rowman & Littlefield, 2018. | Includes bibliographical
   references and index.
Identifiers: LCCN 2017051583 (print) | LCCN 2017053314 (ebook) | ISBN
   9781538108901 (electronic) | ISBN 9781538108895 (hardback : alk. paper)
Subjects: LCSH: Fake news. | Journalism—History—21st century. | Online
   journalism.
Classification: LCC PN4784.F27 (ebook) | LCC PN4784.F27 B37 2018 (print) |
   DDC 070.4/3—dc23
LC record available at https://lccn.loc.gov/2017051583

Printed in the United States of America

To my lovely family:
Alexandra, Emily, Tess, and Caroline.
Love to you all.

Contents

Preface

WHY READ A BOOK BY A LIBRARIAN?

As a topic of debate and discussion, fake news really blew up during the homestretch of the 2016 US presidential election. A search of the *New York Times* database from July 1, 2016, to December 31, 2016, turns up 319 articles in which the phrase *fake news* appears. An identical search covering the same time span turns up 151 such articles in the *Wall Street Journal*. Tallying up the number of social media posts about fake news during the last half of 2016 is impossible, but all the evidence points to the fact that the topic was as big on social media as it was in the traditional news media. And remains so.

At the time when now-familiar phrases such as *fake news* and *alternative facts* started regularly appearing in the media (social and news), at least part of the population reacted with surprise if not shock. For me, however, the stories about fake news came as no surprise. As someone who has worked as an academic librarian since 1990 (and who, prior to that, spent four years teaching research-based college writing), teaching people to think critically about how they evaluate, internalize, and apply information has been a major part of my job for most of my working life. Information literacy is something I have pondered, studied, practiced, and written about for going on three decades.

For those not familiar with the jargon of the library profession, *information literacy* (a phrase that was coined in 1974)[1] describes the efforts of librarians to help people think critically about what they read, hear, and see. Of course, even before the phrase *information literacy* entered the professional lexicon, librarians were actively engaged in teaching people how to negotiate increasingly complex information environments. Evidence exists of library instruction dating back to the 1820s at Harvard University.[2] Courses on using libraries emerged at a number of colleges and universities after the Civil War. Until well into the twentieth century, however, librarians largely focused their instructional efforts on giving tours of library buildings and teaching the use of the local card catalog. Beginning in the 1960s, the role of librarians in instruction was broadened due to such factors as increases in the sheer size of library collections; the emergence of such technologies as microfilm, photocopiers, and classroom projection; and new educational emphases on active-learning techniques like self-directed learning and group participation. Rather than teaching people how to locate items in a given library, practitioners of information literacy recognized that all learners must be equipped with the transferable skills required to identify, organize, and cite information. Even more importantly, information literacy embraced teaching people how to critically evaluate the credibility and appropriateness of information sources; as it turns out, information literacy has always been about teaching the very skills a person needs to navigate today's complex information landscape, a landscape that includes wide swaths of fake news.

In the digital world, information literacy is a far more complex subject than in those times when almost all information came in a physical package of one form or another. Before the web really caught on in the mid to late 1990s, the average person's hunting ground for information was located entirely in the nondigital world and, by the standards of the twenty-first century, was rather limited: subscriptions to a local newspaper and perhaps a handful of national magazines, whatever books were included in one's personal library, the content of television and radio broadcasts, plus the collections of the nearest academic or public libraries. In so limited a universe of information, achieving information literacy—while still a challenge—was less daunting than it is in a digital world where information overload is the one constant, and the old standards of objectivity and factuality seem to have been tossed into the same waste bin containing the pay phone and the foldable road map.

Anyone who wishes to make sense of so crowded and chaotic a landscape would do well to seek out a seasoned guide. Perhaps a guide like me: an information professional who started his career in a nondigital world, transitioned to the digital world, and has devoted thousands of hours to helping people like you become independent, information-literate thinkers.

THE IMPACT OF FAKE NEWS ON INFORMATION LITERACY

As a librarian and an author, I see the explosion of interest in fake news as both a blessing and a curse. The blessing is that the interest in fake news has created a great opportunity for teaching people to become more information literate. Historically, schools and colleges have treated information literacy as something of an orphan subject, never providing it with the type of permanent administrative home enjoyed by service courses like freshman writing or introductory mathematics. As the domain of librarians rather than teaching faculty, full-fledged courses in information literacy have been few; instead, information literacy was something for the librarians to "cover" during a fifty-minute visit with a freshman writing course full of unmotivated students, most of whom did not understand that what the librarian was yakking about had the potential to improve both their grades and their lives. Since fake news (the topic) started making headlines, however, the situation has improved, with interest in information literacy hitting new highs.[3] Colleges and universities are suddenly offering courses on fake news, including for-credit courses taught by nonlibrarian faculty. Outside of educational institutions, ordinary people are seeking guidance on how to sort out trustworthy information from the torrent of unreliable chatter. Truth is, this book would not exist if the fake news phenomenon had not created a demand that the publisher of this book believes will translate into sales and profits.

The fake news phenomenon is also, in some ways, a curse. For one thing, fake news became—almost instantly—an extraordinarily politicized term with multiple meanings. This makes approaching fake news from anything like an objective point of view almost impossible. In January 2017 I published what I intended to be a fairly objective article on the topic of fake news only to immediately see comments accusing me of political bias.[4] Perhaps the worst outcome of the fake news phenomenon would be if all the sound and fury surrounding it turns out to be nothing more than a flavor-of-the-month moral panic that is forgotten as soon as the world turns its attention to the next cause or crisis to come barreling down the path. What would be most unfortunate about such an outcome is that the need to be information literate is not going away just because the hubbub over fake news happens to fade. The problem of untrustworthy information will always be with us. Untrustworthy information existed long before the birth of social media platforms that are not yet old enough to get a driver's license (much less buy a drink), and it will likely be around for centuries after those platforms have been forgotten by all but the most dedicated historians of technology.

ORGANIZATION AND PURPOSE

Chapter 1 of this book begins with a hypothetical example: What if social media as we know it in 2017 had existed in 1964, the year the surgeon general of the United States released his report on the health impacts of smoking? Would the success society has enjoyed in improving human health through reduced smoking have survived a full-on social media onslaught, or would the antismoking efforts of the last fifty years have never gotten off the ground? This then leads to a consideration of why making decisions on the basis of good information matters—in spite of the fact that information, as a human creation, has its limits. Chapter 2 provides definitions and examples (historical and contemporary) of propaganda and fake news and considers what aspects of the fake news phenomenon are actually new versus those which have been around since long before the Digital Age. This chapter also describes how technology can be used to create deceptive information. Chapter 3 describes some of the most common tricks used to pass off deceptive information as credible, while chapter 4 focuses on the misuse of logical fallacies. Chapter 5 lists and illustrates nine questions everyone should ask when evaluating information. Chapter 6 looks at how statistics are used to illuminate as well as to obfuscate and offers practical suggestions for understanding credible statistics and spotting the misuse of statistical information. Chapter 7 examines the special case of scholarly information, covering the (often underappreciated) importance of scholarly information, the basics of the scientific method, and the strengths and weaknesses of scholarly information. Finally, chapter 8 lists and describes online tools to help information seekers evaluate the credibility of the information they encounter.

The intention of this book is to transcend the current furor over fake news by providing readers with durable techniques for evaluating information in almost any form and for almost any purpose, whether it be educational, personal, or professional. If I do my job well, nobody will look at this book ten years from now and say, "Oh, that's so 2017." While writing this book, I endeavored to take as objective an approach as is humanly possible, understanding that perfect objectivity is not possible. It is certainly not my intention to paint any one group as the villains of the fake news phenomenon. As a student of the history of information, I know all too well that lies, exaggerations, and deception are not the exclusive domain of any one party, creed, or calling. There is plenty of blame to go around. My hope is that by having written a book that is worthy of the reader's trust, this book will appeal to, and serve well, anyone who cares about the trustworthiness of the information they encounter, including parents and teachers who want to help children become information-literate students and citizens.

Acknowledgments

I would like to thank all of my library colleagues around the world for their dedication to providing those they serve with access to information and for their efforts in helping people evaluate the information that informs their academic, professional, personal, and civic lives.

Thank you, Caroline, for reading the chapters as I wrote them and for your brilliant advice and clearheaded insight (especially regarding statistics).

1

Credible Information

Why It Matters,
What Are Its Limitations

FAKE NEWS TO THE FORE

On December 3, 2016, a twenty-eight-year-old man from North Carolina walked into a Washington, DC, pizza parlor, pointed a rifle at an employee, and then fired three shots (none of which hit anyone.)[1] He wasn't trying to rob the place. Following his arrest, the man told police he was investigating a conspiracy theory that claimed (without the backing of even one shred of credible evidence) that Hillary Clinton was running a child sex ring out of the restaurant. That particular conspiracy theory was one of many fanned by a worldwide fake news phenomenon. By the final months of 2016, fake news itself had grown to become one of the biggest non–fake news stories of the year.

While the phrase *fake news* rose to prominence in 2016, fake news is really just the latest name for the ancient art of lying. Since the dawn of language, humans have used lies for many purposes: blaming, persuading, winning arguments, exerting dominance. Lying can even be used as a form of entertainment, as evidenced by the many forms of comedy—such as tall tales, pranks, and absurdist humor—that depend on the bending or breaking of the truth. To lie is, in essence, to supply others with misinformation. Fake news, lies, rumors, fibs, propaganda—all are synonyms for misinformation. The consequences of misinformation can range from the trivial (because your car's GPS system slightly misinformed you about the best route to your destination, you drove a mile farther than necessary), to the alarming (three bullet holes in a pizza joint and a lot of terrified citizens), to the tragic (more than once in human history, propaganda has begotten genocide).

If anything good has come from the recent furor over fake news, it is that fake news has highlighted the importance of making sure that the information we take in and, especially, the information we share is credible. Perhaps more than at any time in history, people are at least discussing the importance of evaluating information before allowing it to drive their decisions, whether those decisions be who to vote for, what car to buy, or whether it is a good idea to take a rifle into a pizza parlor in the pursuit of imaginary pedophiles.

EVALUATING INFORMATION: AN ESSENTIAL SKILL IN THE DIGITAL AGE

Centuries from now it is likely that people will refer to the age in which we live as the Digital Age, just as we refer to earlier ages by such names as the Industrial Revolution, the Age of Enlightenment, and the Stone Age. The reason for this, of course, is that digital technology has so filled today's world with information as to make information the defining characteristic of the times in which we live. Millions now make their living working with information, just as millions once made their living working with raw materials like steel or wood. In the twenty-first century, even production-oriented fields like agriculture, mining, and manufacturing employ modern information technology to improve productivity and increase profits. While living in a world filled with easily accessible information can be a wonderful thing, the problem for people who must use information to make important decisions impacting their private and public lives is that not all the information is credible. The challenge, therefore, for those of us living in the Digital Age is to develop skills for evaluating information, the skills for separating information that is credible enough to be useful from that which is not. Helping readers develop the skills for evaluating information is, in a nutshell, the purpose of this book.

SMOKING AND HEALTH:
AN ALTERNATIVE HISTORY

Imagine that you are a resident of the United States and that the date is Saturday, January 11, 1964. Less than two months have passed since the shocking assassination of President John F. Kennedy in Dallas, Texas. It is almost certain that you know about the assassination due to the heavy coverage it received in both the print and broadcast media. In particular, the coverage of the assassination by the national television networks—of which there are only three—was unprecedented in its depth.

In about a month from this date in 1964, the Beatles will appear on the *Ed Sullivan Show* for the first time. US news coverage of the Beatles has been, thus far, so scant that it is quite possible the names John, Paul, George, and Ringo mean nothing to you. Not yet, anyway.

What stands out about this particular Saturday is that Luther Terry, the surgeon general of the United States, has chosen it to release a 387-page document entitled *Smoking and Health: Report of the Advisory Committee to the Surgeon General of the United States.*[2] Though not the first nor the last scientific report on the harmful effects of smoking, *Smoking and Health* emphatically and authoritatively connects the dots between smoking and a number of serious health conditions, including emphysema, heart disease, low birth weight, and lung cancer. Terry opts for a Saturday release so as to not cause any ripples in the stock markets. A Saturday release also ensures that the report will be covered in the Sunday newspapers, an important source of information for Americans in 1964.

Now imagine further that the digital technology of 2016 had existed on the day *Smoking and Health* was released. How might social media and other forms of digital communication respond?

Even before anyone has had time to read the entire report, *Smoking and Health* is being mocked as a nanny-government affront to individual liberty. Tweets and Facebook posts lead the attack (see figures 1.1 and 1.2). Satirical memes soon follow (figure 1.3).

Next are the many click-bait news stories with enticing headlines like

> Have You Seen the Ten Reasons Why Cigarettes Cannot Possibly Cause Cancer? You'll Be Amazed. . . .

> Five False Conclusions Contained in the Surgeon General's Report. Smoke Out the Facts. . . .

Within a few weeks, pro-smoking activists are promoting a heavily edited attack video in which US Public Health Service staff appear to admit that the surgeon general's report is based on fake science and the connection between smoking and cancer is a complete fabrication. Even though the video is thoroughly discredited, it receives over five hundred thousand views on YouTube while generating tens of thousands of disparaging comments from outraged smokers.

Likes to Smoke
@Smokey

Follow

FAKE GOVERNMENT SCIENCE: Lies come twenty to the pack in Surgeon General's "report" on smoking.

#FakeScience #SmokingisSafe

5:53 PM - 11 January 1964 - Washington, DC, United States

↰   ↳ 9,368   ✳ 997

FIGURE 1.1
Tweeting about *Smoking and Health. National Archives photograph.*

FIGURE 1.2
A Facebook user weighs in. *New York Public Library photo. U.S. Government Document.*

FIGURE 1.3
The surgeon general gets the meme treatment. *Donald A. Barclay*

Howard Cullman, a director of the Philip Morris company, bluntly says of the findings published in *Smoking and Health*, "We don't accept the idea that there are harmful agents in tobacco."[3] Soon, ostensibly scientific articles reporting results contradicting the conclusions of *Smoking and Health* begin to appear in "predatory journals"—nominally scientific, online-only journals that will publish almost anything in exchange for payment. While at first glance these articles appear to be legitimate, they are not based on genuine scientific research and their findings are either exaggerated or simply made up. Many suspect that Big Tobacco is secretly funding both the wave of fake scientific articles and a good part of the social-media churn slamming the surgeon general's report. Some accuse Big Tobacco of using machine-generated tweets and Facebook posts to make the opposition to *Smoking and Health* seem more widespread than it actually is.

Because 1964 is an election year, both houses of Congress respond to the growing digital uproar by holding hearings. During testimony, representatives and senators from tobacco-growing states, as well as their colleagues who receive campaign financing from Big Tobacco, are especially hostile to the surgeon general and the team of medical advisers who contributed to *Smoking and Health*. Sensing an opportunity, presidential candidate Barry Goldwater (a lifelong nonsmoker) repeatedly denounces the link between cancer and smoking as a communist-inspired hoax. With an eye on the opinion polls, President Lyndon Johnson (an on-again, off-again smoker) distances his administration from the surgeon general's report, choosing instead to expend his political capital on addressing the growing crisis in Vietnam and shepherding civil rights legislation through the House and Senate. After all the uproar, *Smoking and Health* is filed away and forgotten. Across the country and around the world, cigarette smokers cough sighs of relief.

Of course, there was no digital social media in 1964. Rather than being filed away and forgotten, the scientific findings reported in

Smoking and Health were widely accepted (in spite of the best efforts of Big Tobacco to spread disinformation and discredit legitimate scientific research). Thanks to the many antismoking initiatives launched in the wake of *Smoking and Health*, the United States saw smoking rates for adults drop from 42.4 percent in 1965 (the peak year for smoking in the United States) to 16.8 percent in 2014.[4] The transformation of cigarette smoking from an accepted part of daily life to a borderline-taboo habit was a major public health victory that directly led to millions of people living longer, healthier lives while saving the nation billions in health care costs associated with smoking and secondhand smoke.[5] Even among present-day smokers, it is hard to find anyone who believes it would have been for the best if the scientific facts championed by *Smoking and Health* had been buried under a landslide of uninformed popular opinion. And while there are those who believe smoking is an individual choice that should not be controlled by government regulations, very few actively long for a society in which the population still smokes like it was 1964.

The box contains an exercise in alternative history; the point of this indulgence is simple: facts and truth matter. Information matters. Matters enough that it can change the world. Though some glibly claim that we now live in a "post-truth world," the reality is that if human beings, both as individuals and as members of a larger society, are going to make the best possible decisions regarding just about everything that affects their lives, they had better base these decision on credible information rather than on wishful thinking, fantasies, or outright falsehoods.

INFORMATION, DECISION MAKING, AND PRACTICAL REASON

The study of information is a broad and complex topic with branches reaching into such academic fields as computer science, philosophy, and the social sciences. Something as seemingly straightforward as the definition of information is, in fact, complex and controversial enough to spark intense philosophical debates. The approach throughout this book, however, is to consider information through the lens of *practical reason*, which has been defined as "the general human capacity for resolving, through reflection, the question of what one is to do."[6] Through this lens, the practical purpose of information can be seen as helping human beings decide what to do and, by extension, what to believe. While in some ways such an approach to information is overly simplistic, it lends itself to the real-world needs of information seekers who are trying to make the best possible decisions based on the best possible information.

INFORMATION AND THE INCIDENT COMMANDER

For a dramatic example of the way credible information informs decision making, consider the case of a professional firefighter who has been appointed the incident commander (i.e., the person in charge) of a growing wildfire. The fire has already spread to two thousand acres on a hot and windy summer day, and in order to safely and effectively respond to this fire, the incident commander must make the best possible decisions based on accurate and up-to-date information touching on a number of factors:

- The fire's current perimeter and rate of spread
- Topography of the area in which the fire is burning
- Amount, types, and dryness of the fuel in the area
- Current and expected weather conditions
- Location of roads, structures, and water sources

- Whereabouts of civilians and firefighters
- The type and number of firefighting resources currently available, additional resources on the way, and when those additional resources will arrive

While this is just a partial list of information an incident commander needs, it dramatically illustrates the fact that good decision making calls for credible information. If, for example, an incident commander were falsely informed that a fire was burning in sparse grass on flat ground when it was actually burning in heavy chaparral on a 60 percent slope, any decisions based on that faulty information could be disastrous, possibly even fatal, for firefighters and civilians alike.

SOME REALITIES OF INFORMATION

Becoming adept at evaluating information means understanding and accepting the fact that information, though powerful, has its limits. As a product of human thought and human effort, information is often problematic and always less than perfect. Anyone who approaches the evaluation of information with the idea that any information that falls short of perfection must be rejected is bound to be disappointed.

With that in mind, the realities of information described in the following pages are

- the credibility continuum
- information, knowledge, and skill
- tricky facts
- information, interpretation, and opinion
- the expertise factor

The Credibility Continuum

For the purposes of evaluating information, it is vital to understand that credibility exists on a continuum rather than in separate spheres of true and false information. Indeed, those who approach the evaluation of information with a binary mind-set—"It's either true or it's false, no middle ground"—are setting themselves up for failure.

You will sometimes hear people speak of "bad information." That phrase is problematic because thinking of information as either bad or good is overly simplistic. Yes, there is bad information of the sort that is completely made up out of whole cloth:

- Albert Einstein invented the xylophone.
- The fourth letter of the English alphabet is *z*.
- The sun rises in the west and sets in the east.

And, yes, there is good information that is as 100 percent truthful as anything created by fallible humanity can be:

- The speed of light is 186,000 miles per second.
- π, the ratio of a circle's circumference to its diameter, is approximated at 3.14.
- Maya Angelou was born in St. Louis, Missouri, in 1928.

If all information fit neatly into the categories of "good information" (completely true) and "bad information" (completely false), then evaluating information would be relatively easy. The problem is that we inhabit a world in which vast amounts of information fall somewhere in between the two extremes of the credibility continuum. The challenge facing anyone evaluating information is not, in most cases, deciding between true or false, but rather where on the credibility continuum a piece of information lies and, in the end, deciding when any given piece of information is credible enough to fulfill a given information need.

THREE COMMON INFORMATION FRUSTRATIONS

Information can frustrate in a number of ways. The three frustrations listed here are so common that almost anyone who seeks information is bound to encounter them, usually sooner rather than later.

Intentionally Falsified Information

Human beings intentionally create false information. This, in essence, is what the fake news furor is all about. The reasons for intentionally creating false information vary widely. German industrialist Oskar Schindler famously falsified information to save the lives of Jewish inmates of Nazi concentration camps. Stockbroker Bernard Madoff notoriously falsified information to defraud thousands of investors. *The Onion* creates fake news stories for comedic purposes (and to earn advertising revenues). The list of reasons for intentionally creating false information goes on and on. Whatever the motivation of its creators, intentionally false information has the potential to sow confusion and spread misinformation.

Unintentionally False Information

False information can be created unintentionally. For example, someone may honestly believe with every fiber of their being that they saw Elvis singing to Bigfoot at a rest stop on Interstate 40; however, sincerity of belief does not make their Facebook post reporting Elvis in concert with Bigfoot a credible source of information. For a real-world example, there is the case of two physicists at the University of Utah who, in 1989, claimed to have produced energy using tabletop cold fusion and subsequently published a scientific paper outlining their methodology and results.[7] If the physicists' findings about cold fusion were correct, it would mean limitless clean energy for the entire world. However, no other scientists were ever able to replicate the results documented by paper's authors and the research has been discredited. There is no evidence that the two physicists who conducted the experiment and published the paper were trying to deceive anyone; they simply made an error when measuring their results. Should they have been more careful? Yes. Were they being dishonest? No. Does it make any difference if the false information that misleads you was created by mistake rather than by intent? Not really.

Information That Is Not There

It can be extremely frustrating to learn that information you would very much like to have simply does not exist. Information is not a naturally occurring substance like oxygen or water. Unless someone has made a record of *something* by writing it down, drawing it, mapping it, capturing it on camera, entering it into a database, or otherwise recording it in a fixed format, the information about that *something* will not exist. A scholar who studies the history of slavery might very much wish for a database containing the age, sex, birth name, place of origin, native language, and tribal affiliation of every person ever forced onto a slave ship and transported from Africa to the New World. While that information could exist in theory, it does not exist in fact. Why? Because the data was never recorded in the first place. Those who profited from the slave trade could have recorded all that information—and a lot more—about the unfortunate individuals caught up in the horror of human slavery, but they did not put themselves to the trouble. A more modern example of missing information is the case of statistics on police shootings in the United States. Because local police agencies are not required to submit data on police shootings to the US Bureau of Justice Statistics, there is a dearth of reliable statistics on police shootings in the United States even though many people would like to have that information for both current and past years.[8]

A second reason for missing information is that the permanent record of the information has been destroyed. The destruction of the Great Library of Alexandria (which was likely due to a series of events starting in the first century BCE and ending in the seventh century BCE rather than a single cataclysmic sacking and burning) is often cited as one of the greatest losses of information in human history, in part because almost every item in the Library of Alexandria was unique. For a more recent example of lost information, the original high-quality videotapes of the Apollo 11 moon landing were lost after having been erased and reused, leaving only a low-quality video record of the landing.[9]

A third reason that desired, potentially valuable information is missing is that it is unobtainable by human beings, either permanently or thus far. An example of permanently unobtainable information is the data that could be acquired through the study of living specimens of extinct dinosaur species. An example of information that might someday be obtained, but which has so far eluded humanity, would be the formula for a cheap, safe, and effective cure for the common cold.

A fourth reason that desired information is not available is that it is a secret. Information could be a government secret, such as classified information concerning the activities of the police or military. Information could take the form of a corporate secret, such as the rigorously guarded formula for making Coca-Cola. Or the information could be a personal secret known to only one or just a few individuals who refuse to divulge it. An example of the latter is the identity of the Watergate informant known as Deep Throat. After being kept secret for decades by *Washington Post* reporters Bob Woodward and Carl Bernstein, the real identity of Deep Throat was revealed by a family attorney to be former Federal Bureau of Investigation assistant director Mark Felt, who by the time his identity was revealed was suffering from dementia and near death.[10]

Information, Knowledge, and Skill

The plot of *Star Wars: Episode IV: A New Hope*, the original film in the *Star Wars* saga, hinges on information. Possession of the plans for (i.e., information about) the dreaded Death Star drives all the action of the film. But what if those plans had been in a code the rebels did not have the knowledge to break? What if the rebels had not possessed the engineering knowledge to identify from those plans the Death Star's one weakness? What if Luke Skywalker lacked the skill (or, more accurately, space magic) to bulls-eye the Death Star's Achilles' exhaust port and send the fans of the film home happy? Any of these shortcomings on the rebel side would have resulted in a very different outcome and a very different movie. And the point? Merely possessing information is not enough to make practical use of it.

Considering the more down-to-earth example of the wildfire mentioned earlier, merely having access to credible information is not, by itself, enough to result in a successful fire-suppression effort. It requires the knowledge (acquired through education and training) and the skill (acquired through practice and experience) of the incident commander—along with the knowledge and skills of everyone involved in fighting the fire—to translate information about topography, weather, firefighting resources, and so on into a successful fire-suppression effort. If, say, a singer from the Metropolitan Opera were put in charge of a wildfire and supplied with the exact same information supplied to the incident commander, it is extremely unlikely that the outcome would be a successful fire-suppression effort. The average opera singer simply lacks the knowledge or experience—lacks the *expertise*—to interpret and correctly respond to highly technical firefighting information. For example, while the fact that the area in which a fire is burning has a Haines Index of 5 is significant to an incident commander's decision-making process, that same information most likely means nothing to an accomplished professional singer who has devoted years to mastering arias but no time at all to the study of wildland fire suppression. Even if our hypothetical singer actually understood the significance of a Haines Index of 5, that knowledge by itself is not enough to transform a singer into an incident commander capable of making sound decisions based on information about the fire.

Turning the tables, assume the incident commander and the opera star were both handed an identical set of information: the words and music to Puccini's aria "Un Bel di Vedremo." Even if the incident commander has the knowledge required to read the musical notes on the page, it is incredibly unlikely that he or she possesses the skill required to sing the aria at a high level of artistry. The Metropolitan Opera star, on the other hand, would be entirely likely to have both the knowledge and the skill (let's assume our singer is a soprano) to render the aria at the level expected of professional singers.

It is easy to come up with many examples demonstrating why the application of information requires knowledge and skill. Someone with no medical training could have access to every bit of information required to conduct a heart transplant, but without the knowledge to fully understand that information and the skill to turn the information into action (not to mention millions of dollars' worth of medical gear), a successful heart transplant is not going to happen. Complete information about how to fly a 747 does not automatically turn the person who possesses it into a competent airline pilot, especially if that information is in a language the would-be pilot cannot read. Information about an academic subject is vital to the scholar, but making effective use of that information requires both the knowledge to understand the information and the skill to organize and communicate that understanding in the form of a written document or an oral presentation.

Tricky Facts

The fictional character of Sergeant Joe Friday from the *Dragnet* radio/television/movie franchise is famously associated with the catchphrase "Just the facts, ma'am." Those who struggle to evaluate the credibility of information get Friday's point. Why can't all information be boiled down to just the essential facts? Nobody wants equivocations, ifs, or nuances—give us definitive, rock-solid facts. As frustrating as it may be, the truth is that complicated questions about complicated topics do not lend themselves to simple answers. And while facts constitute the crucially important building blocks of credible information, facts by themselves are not sufficient to address complicated questions. To better understand why this is so, it is important to understand how the sometimes-slippery nature of facts can limit their authoritativeness.

Without zooming off into stratospheric epistemological debates, for the practical purpose of evaluating information it is reasonable to say that facts are things that are correct or that have occurred. For something to be a fact, it needs to be verifiable through some rational process such as gathering evidence, testing, observation, measurement, experience, and so on.

Let's do a fact check. How would you answer this multiple-choice question?

The length meter is equal to

A. 10 millimeters
B. 1,000 millimeters
C. 10,000 millimeters

Even if 97 percent of the people reading this book chose answer A (10 millimeters) or C (10,000 millimeters), the correct answer is, nonetheless, B (1,000 millimeters). That the length of 1 meter is equal to 1,000 millimeters is a fact that no amount of arguing, political activism, or beseeching of the heavens is going to change.

The type of fact represented by "1 meter equals 1,000 millimeters" is an *incontrovertible fact*. Incontrovertible facts are so well substantiated and so widely accepted that rejecting them amounts to irrationality. The world is filled with incontrovertible facts:

- The atomic number of the element carbon is 6.
- Most coffee is grown in the equatorial regions of the world.
- John Milton's *Paradise Lost* begins with the words, "Of Man's First Disobedience . . ."

Though incontrovertible facts may be plentiful, not everything presented as a fact is necessarily an incontrovertible fact. Indeed, when someone presents a piece of information as if it were an incontrovertible fact—as politicians and pundits are fond of doing—it should immediately sound an alarm and raise the question, "Is that fact really incontrovertible? Is it really so true that it cannot be denied or disputed?" Incontrovertible is, after all, the highest possible standard to which any fact can be held.

More common than incontrovertible facts are *conditional facts*. For example, "Water boils at 100° Celsius (212° Fahrenheit)" is a conditional fact because, while that statement is true, it is only true so long as the atmospheric pressure equals one atmosphere (the atmospheric pressure—with slight variations—at sea level). Because most of the world lives at altitudes where

COMMON KNOWLEDGE

Common knowledge is any fact so well-known and so widely accepted as the truth that the average knowledgeable, educated reader would know it without having to look it up. What constitutes common knowledge can vary from one group to another. For example, while the fact that Antonio José de Sucre was Bolivia's first elected president would be considered common knowledge in Bolivia, it is not considered common knowledge in the United States—unless you happen to be communicating with a US audience made up of people who study the history of South America. Similarly, Boyle's law (the pressure of a gas increases as the size of the container decreases) would be considered common knowledge when communicating with most scientists and engineers but probably not when communicating with a general audience. An example of common knowledge that need not be cited in any situation appears earlier in this chapter: 1,000 millimeters equal 1 meter.

Another characteristic of common knowledge is that multiple reference sources define or describe it in the same way. In formal academic writing, it is not necessary to cite anything that is considered common knowledge, though it is a good idea to cite a source if there is a chance that something might not be common knowledge to your intended audience.

the boiling point of water is close enough to the sea-level boiling point so as to not make much of an impact on everyday life, people tend to think of the 100° Celsius figure as an incontrovertible fact even though it is merely conditional. In the high-altitude environs of Denver, Colorado, for example, the boiling point of water drops to approximately 95° Celsius (203° Fahrenheit), forcing residents there to adjust cooking times in order to ensure that foods are thoroughly cooked. Another type of a conditional fact is one that changes over time or varies from country to country. Trained musicians know as fact that the musical note A above middle C (the note the oboe plays when an orchestra tunes up) has a frequency of 440 Hz. While this is true today, 440 Hz wasn't standardized until 1939 and previous to being standardized varied from place to place and over time.[11]

There are also *pseudo facts*. Pseudo facts are things widely assumed to be facts when they are not. One example of a pseudo fact is the attribution of the catchphrase "Just the facts, ma'am" to Sgt. Joe Friday (referred to earlier). In the entirety of *Dragnet*'s run on radio and television, Friday never uttered the exact words, "Just the facts, ma'am." That particular wording was actually popularized by a parody recording entitled "St. George and the Dragonet."[12] Yet another example of a pseudo fact: There was a time when schoolchildren in the United States were routinely taught that the crew of Christopher Columbus's expedition of 1492 were the first Europeans to visit the New World. Some may still believe this to be true. However, archaeological evidence has conclusively proven that Vikings were sailing to, and establishing settlements in, the New World hundreds of years before Columbus set out from Spain.[13] A more factual statement would be, "The expeditions of Christopher Columbus ultimately led to the establishment of the first *permanent* European settlements in the New World." (While some of the Viking New World settlements lasted for decades, all were eventually abandoned.)

Of course, *falsehoods* are sometimes presented as facts without being based on any reasonably credible evidence. Example: A small minority of people might assert as fact that Earth is flat; however, based on all reasonable evidence, they might as well assert as fact that 1 meter equals 10,000 milliliters or that the boiling point of water at sea level is $-10°$ Celsius.

Information, Interpretation, and Opinion

The information people are most likely to encounter in their daily lives is typically an interpretation of facts (of varying degrees of certainty) as well as other forms of evidence that, while credible, might not reach the standard of facts. For example, consider the statistics in table 1.1 about baseball greats Willie Mays and Babe Ruth, each of whom happened to have enjoyed a Major League Baseball career that lasted exactly twenty-two seasons.

FACTS ARE STUBBORN THINGS

One of the most famous quotations about facts comes from John Adams, the second president of the United States:

> Facts are stubborn things; and whatever may be our wishes, our inclinations, or the dictates of our passion, they cannot alter the state of facts and evidence.

Yes, facts are stubborn—if and when they are truly incontrovertible facts. Too often, things presented as facts turn out to be a more slippery than solid, as in the example of the boiling point of water. So what about the Adams quotation? Is it really a fact that John Adams said, "Facts are stubborn things"? Yes, it is a fact—at least as far as it is reasonably possible to prove. A contemporary court document reports Adams using the previously quoted sentence during his successful defense of a group of British soldiers standing trial for murder in the wake of the Boston Massacre.[14] The existence of that court document constitutes strongly convincing evidence.

Is the evidence convincing enough for us to conclude that Adams's use of "Facts are stubborn things" is an incontrovertible fact? While the evidence comes close to that standard, it does not quite reach the level of absolute certainty. Because the court document is the only known source for Adams's use of the phrase, this leaves open the remote possibility that the words appearing in the court document were incorrectly recorded or intentionally falsified or in one way or another jumbled somewhere between the time of the trial itself and the actual meeting of inked type and paper. But even if we cannot conclude it is an incontrovertible fact that Adams said, "Facts are stubborn things," the available evidence ranks so high on the credibility scale that the most reasonable conclusion is that Adams said those words as shown in the court document.

Digging a bit deeper, if you type "Facts are stubborn things" into a web search engine, you will retrieve a large number of sources citing Adams's use of the phrase. As a result, it may seem reasonable to conclude that the phrase originated with Adams. But is it really a fact that Adams was the first person to say, "Facts are stubborn things"? Absolutely not. There are many printed examples of the use of the phrase "Facts are stubborn things" that predate the Boston Massacre trial, with the earliest known example dating back to 1713—twenty-two years before Adams was born.[15] Given the preponderance of evidence, it is an incontrovertible fact that John Adams was not the first person to use the phrase "Facts are stubborn things." For it to be otherwise would require an unbelievably complex and improbable set of circumstances, quite possibly involving time travel and multiple conspiracies.

Finally, in a web search of "Facts are stubborn things" you may also come across references to President Ronald Reagan's use of the phrase "Facts are stupid things" during his address to the 1988 Republican National Convention in New Orleans. Is this a fact? Did Ronald Reagan, as president of the United States, really say in a public address "Facts are stupid things?" Yes, he said it. It is a thoroughly documented fact. However, it is also a fact that Reagan immediately corrected his misstatement to say, "Facts are stubborn things." In addition, he correctly used the phrase "Facts are stubborn things" a total of six times in the course of his speech.[16] So while it is factual for critics of Reagan to claim that he publicly said "Facts are stupid things," it would be dishonest of them to point to this fact, in and of itself, as conclusive evidence that Reagan believed facts are stupid.

Facts are facts, but they don't necessarily add up to the truth, especially when used selectively or with the intent to deceive.

Table 1.1. Career Statistics of Willie Mays and Babe Ruth

Career Statistics	Willie Mays	Babe Ruth
Batting average	.302	.342
Hits	3,283	2,873
Home runs	660	714
Runs batted in	1,903	2,213
Stolen bases	338	123

The numbers in table 1.1 are, beyond any reasonable doubt, facts. However, those facts cannot definitively answer a basic question: "Who was the better baseball player, Willie Mays or Babe Ruth?" Any attempt to answer that question requires some interpretation of the facts.

Supporters of Ruth will point out that he had more career home runs and RBIs than Mays as well as a higher career batting average. Fan of Mays will counter with the fact that Mays had more career hits and nearly three times as many stolen bases as Ruth in spite of sacrificing—during the prime of his playing days—the opportunity to play in 266 Major League Baseball games due to his service in the US Army. That may be, the Ruthians will respond, but Ruth was not only a homerun-slugging outfielder, he was also a skilled pitcher who amassed a very respectable 94–46 win-loss record along with a career earned run average of 2.28.

As with many debates, the argument shifts from points that can be proven with facts to points supported by evidence that, while credible, requires some interpretation. For example, those who favor Mays will point to his amazing skills as a defensive outfielder. Though, almost without exception, baseball historians and experts agree that Mays was one of the all-time-best defensive outfielders while Ruth was merely average to good in the outfield, this is not a point that can be proven by hard numbers in the way that "Who hit more home runs?" or "Who accumulated the most hits?" can be proven by numbers. The complex components of what makes someone a great defensive outfielder—knowledge of opposing hitters, ability to read balls off the bat, speed, ability to catch and throw the ball—cannot be fully conveyed through historical baseball statistics.

The Ruth versus Mays argument can go on forever and is, ultimately, unwinnable.[17] There are countless examples of similar arguments that, while fueled by facts and other credible evidence, can never be definitively won. An example from military history is the "lions led by donkeys" theory of World War I. According to this theory, the soldiers of the British Army fought like lions while their generals behaved like donkeys, indiscriminately wasting the lives of their troops by refusing to abandon outdated tactics when confronted with the terrible realities of the twentieth century's industrial-scale warfare. While similarly cynical views of British military leadership and strategy had been circulating since the time of World War I itself, the lions led by donkeys theory came dominate mainstream thinking among historians in the early 1960s. As time when on, however, some historians began countering the then-dominant lions/donkeys theory by arguing that British military leadership was not incompetent; that British commanders, far from being blindly devoted to outdated tactics, changed their tactics as the war progressed and learned to improvise in response to dynamic battlefield situations. It is likely that historians of World War I will continue to argue their conflicting points for decades, if not centuries, and in doing so will use numerical facts (casualty rates, number of shells fired, number of machine guns per battalion, etc.) along with other forms of credible evidence (diaries, contemporary military records, historical photographs, archaeological evidence, etc.) to bolster their arguments.

Unwinnable arguments inevitably end up invoking opinions. While it is common to dismiss opinion-supported arguments as "just an opinion" (especially when those opinions contradict our own), well-informed opinions do carry weight and need to be considered. In the Mays versus Ruth argument, the opinion of, say, a hypothetical baseball professional who has played and coached the game, studied its history, and evaluated thousands of players at every level of professional baseball should carry more weight than the opinion of a casual fan. This is not to say that the opinion of one baseball professional—including our hypothetical expert—is the authoritative, case-closed opinion on Mays versus Ruth, merely that his opinion should be taken seriously and given due consideration along with the opinions of other experts and in light of all the other facts and evidence.

The Expertise Factor

Especially when dealing with topics outside of our immediate areas of knowledge and expertise, we often look to experts for guidance. Perhaps the most frustrating thing about turning to experts for guidance is when the opinions of experts conflict. How are ordinary people supposed to make sense of information when highly educated and experienced experts cannot agree on what it means? A classic example of this occurs when expert witnesses testify in court cases. Say that, during the course of a patent infringement lawsuit, the plaintiff's attorneys swear in a computer scientist who testifies that a key bit of computer code is the property of company M and also asserts that company A clearly purloined the code for use in its new software. It is a safe bet that the defense attorneys will then call to the witness stand an equally well-qualified computer scientist whose testimony contradicts that of the plaintiff's expert. How can this be? There are, in fact, a number of possible explanations:

- Offers of money can cause people, even experts, to bend, if not break, the truth.
- Experts are fallible human beings who sometimes make mistakes or are swayed by their own biases. If experts were infallible, they would always be in agreement.
- An expert may offer an opinion without having access to all the pertinent information. In the court testimony example, the plaintiff's attorneys could have withheld from their hired expert witness information about the allegedly purloined computer code that, if not withheld, might have caused that expert to offer a different opinion in court.
- Finally, some questions are so complex that even experts with vast amounts of training and experience in a specific field of study can disagree on what all the facts and evidence actually mean.

Another point to consider about expertise is to remember that nobody can be an expert in everything. In the 1984 comedy film *The Adventures of Buckaroo Banzai Across the 8th Dimension*, the eponymous protagonist is a neurosurgeon, particle physicist, rock star, and inventor all rolled into a cowboy-themed action hero. Of course, such an outrageous Renaissance man character makes sense only in the goofy context of a film like *Buckaroo Banzai*. In the real world, any one person's area of in-depth expertise tends to be limited to a narrow, highly specialized field. There are exceptions, but these exceptions stand out because they are so rare.

What is not so rare is someone with expertise in one field claiming to have expertise in different field, sometimes for less than honorable purposes. And while claims to multispecialty expertise can sometimes be valid, it is not a given that someone with a PhD in mathematics is also an expert in space exploration or nutrition. Nor is a retired navy admiral whose entire career specialization focused on submarine warfare necessarily any more of an expert on infantry tactics than a retired bus driver. Expertise in any field must be earned and demonstrated, not automatically granted as a privilege of education, occupation, or office.

Finally, there are those who have no real training or experience yet somehow pass themselves off experts. Frank Abagnale (whose story was fictionalized in the film *Catch Me If You Can*) successfully passed himself off as a lawyer, physician, pilot, and federal agent. All too often, fake experts end up quoted in news stories or appearing as guests on news programs. For one example, in 2017 a US news network interviewed a man identified as "Sweden's Defense and National Security Adviser" who turned out to have "a criminal record in the United States and no ties to Sweden's security establishment."[18]

"You know everybody is ignorant, only on different subjects."

—*Will Rogers*[19]

Evaluating the credibility of any given expert is a challenging but necessary part of evaluating information. Later chapters in this book will go into more detail on techniques for evaluating individual experts as well as seeking out the consensus opinion of multiple experts.

WHEN IS ENOUGH EVALUATION ENOUGH?

When you encounter information that seems like it will meet your information need, you then must evaluate its credibility. The remaining chapters of this book deal with techniques for how to evaluate information, but for now the question is "How much evaluation do I need to do before deciding if a piece of information is credible?" Because evaluating information requires time and effort, thoroughly evaluating every bit of information you encounter is unrealistic. Instead, the amount of effort you put into evaluating information should be based on your information need and, specifically, on what is at stake in any decisions the information leads you to make.

For example, if you found a wild mushroom and needed to know if it was safe to eat or poisonous, you would be dealing with an extremely high-stakes information need. Under those circumstances, it would make sense to thoroughly evaluate any information telling you that the mushroom was edible instead of simply trusting that information at face value and serving up a potentially deadly fungus for dinner. On the other hand, say you were standing in front of a candy machine and you impulsively decided to purchase an Idaho Spud candy bar. Though you have never tried an Idaho Spud before, you had once seen a random Instagram post declaring it to be "the greatest candy bar in the history of the world." While it is true your purchasing decision would be based on not-very-credible information, the stakes involved are extremely low. The worst outcome is that the Idaho Spud bar turns out to be not to your liking and you have wasted the small amount of money you put into the candy machine.[20] Hardly the end of the world.

Of course, most situations that call for evaluating information fall somewhere between a life-or-death decision and the price of a candy bar. A student who is planning to incorporate information into a paper or presentation will need to decide how much effort to put into evaluating that information based on the importance of the assignment. Logic dictates more thoroughly evaluating information for a major term paper as opposed to information for a nightly homework assignment. A Facebook user who is thinking about sharing a link to an article about the latest political outrage on the part of "those idiots" would do well to make sure the link points to a credible article. If the plan is to share the link with a couple of like-minded friends via direct messaging, the thoroughness of the evaluation process can be less rigorous than when forwarding it to 347 various and sundry Facebook friends. If there is one sure way to quickly find yourself unfriended, it is sharing controversial articles without checking to make sure they are at least minimally credible.

It may help to think of evaluating information in terms of return on investment. If you were diagnosed with a life-threatening medical condition and you invested twenty hours of your time into carefully evaluating the credibility of information concerning potentially lifesaving medical treatments, your return on your investment of those hours could be huge—many additional years of healthy living. In contrast, investing twenty hours into researching the credibility of a post recommending one particular brand of dish soap over another is unlikely to provide any return on your investment.

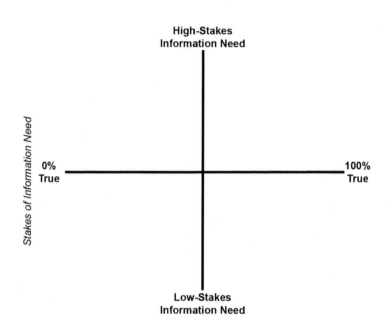

FIGURE 1.4
Balancing credibility with what is at stake if the information proves to be misleading. *Donald A. Barclay*

As there are no formulas for deciding when the credibility of any given piece of information is good enough for any given information need, it is up to the individual to make the call on a case-by-case basis (see figure 1.4). That said, it is hard to imagine why anyone would make even a low-stakes decision on information known to be 100 percent false (or close to it). At the same time, making a high-stakes decision on information that is less than highly credible would be foolhardy. In the end it is about using the highly subjective standard of due diligence when evaluating information, of adjusting the thoroughness of the evaluation to what is at stake in the decision that must be, ultimately, made.

EVALUATING INFORMATION AND BALANCE

As with most things in life, evaluating information works best when you achieve proper balance. On the one extreme, you do not want to become someone who automatically rejects all information that fails to rise to some idealized level of perfection. The effect of such hypervigilant evaluation of information would be to cut yourself off from much of what you stand to learn from the knowledge and experience of others. On the other extreme, there is no benefit to being so gullible as to accept at face value every bit of information that crosses your path. Uncritically accepting information without any evaluation is how people end up falling for online scams or dismaying friends and family by forwarding patently fake Internet rumors. Sometimes, this is how people end up in the back of a Washington, DC, police car facing a host of very serious federal charges.

RECAP

For practical purposes, we can think of information as a crucial element of the decision-making process. In the current Digital Age, the ability to evaluate information is an essential skill.

It is important to understand certain limiting realities of information:

- The credibility of information is rarely a binary true/false proposition. For most information, credibility falls somewhere in between completely false and completely true.
- Making productive use of information requires knowledge and skill. Simply possessing information is not enough if you do not understand the information or know how to make use of it.

- Facts, though a crucial component of credible information, are sometimes tricky things to nail down and do not always tell the whole story.
- Making use of even very credible information often requires interpretation and the incorporation of opinion.
- Expert interpretation and opinion are valuable tools for making sense of information, but the qualifications of experts must be evaluated.

The amount of evaluation any piece of information requires depends on what is at stake. Information that informs important decisions demands more evaluation than information that informs less important decisions. Users of information must practice due diligence in evaluating information.

As important as credible information is to the decisions we make, it is worth remembering that information is a tool, not a magic wand. No matter how credible, timely, or exhaustive any given body or piece of information may be, information by itself cannot cure a disease, improve the economy, or plant a crop. Like all tools, the ultimate value of information depends on both the ability of people to use it and the purposes for which they choose to use it.

In an ideal world, only the most credible information informs public decisions about such important matters as the economy, the environment, justice, education, and national defense. The same holds true for personal decisions about such matters as finance, career choices, health, and child rearing. For students, information drives decisions about how to answer test and homework questions, what to write in essays, and how to develop presentations. Regardless of who is using the information or what they are using it for, democracies, families, and individuals cannot thrive if their important decisions are based on information that is not credible.

Fake News as Phenomenon

(Almost) Nothing New Under the Sun

As previously mentioned, stories about the fake news phenomenon made headlines and blew up on social media during the latter part of 2016. It may be that the furor over fake news is the reason you are reading this book and why you are interested in becoming more skilled at evaluating information. Fake news, though, is one of those troublesome phrases that gets casually tossed around by different people in different ways. In light of this, it is worth taking some time to define our terms.

FAKE NEWS

What is fake news? A seemingly simple question that is not so simple to answer (see figure 2.1).

If you follow the lead of some politicians and their most devoted followers, fake news is defined as "anything that reports something I don't want to believe." This is not an accurate or useful definition of fake news, as it permits the label *fake news* to be applied to information that is highly credible and not at all fake. Employing so subjective and narrow a definition, the government of North Korea could brand as fake news any reports that the people of South Korea lead lives that are more prosperous and freer than those led by the people of North Korea—in spite of the fact that those reports are highly credible and, as far as questions of prosperity and individual freedom go, easily verified. Similarly, an individual who refuses to believe that racism exists in

FIGURE 2.1
The many faces of fake news. *istock/ jax10289*

the United States could label as fake news any reports to the contrary, regardless of whether those reports are credible.

Tossing aside the "anything I don't want to hear" definition, it is fair to ask if fake news is the same thing as propaganda (a topic discussed in detail later). This is a tricky question. Instead of setting off propaganda as something distinct from fake news, it is more accurate to see propaganda as a subset of fake news. As a subset, propaganda is distinguished from other types of fake news in that propaganda is intentionally created to advance a specific political, organizational, or commercial agenda—something that is not true of all fake news.

In the broadest definition, then, fake news is any information that is intentionally created under the pretense that it is credible when, in reality, it is not.

Forms of Fake News

To define fake news, it helps to consider the various forms in which it comes. Of course, there is not universal agreement on what those forms are. Journalist Claire Wardle identifies seven types of "mis and disinformation":

1. Satire or parody
2. Misleading content
3. Imposter content

4. Fabricated content
5. False connection
6. False context
7. Manipulated content[1]

Academics Hunt Allcott and Matthew Gentzkow, who define fake news as "news articles that are intentionally and verifiably false, and could mislead readers," identify fewer types of fake news than does Wardle:

- Intentionally fabricated news articles
- Satirical articles that can be misinterpreted as nonsatirical

They also exclude several "close cousins of fake news" from their definition:

- Unintentional reporting mistakes
- Rumors that are not the product of a specific fake news article
- Conspiracy theories
- Satirical articles that are unlikely to be seen as nonsatirical
- Lies told by politicians
- Information that is slanted or misleading but not completely false[2]

Of course, other scholars and commentators will have their own takes on the various types of fake news. For the purpose of this book, I choose to divide fake news into three broad categories.

Mercenary Fake News

As the name implies, mercenary fake news is created for the purpose of making money with no intent on the part of its creators to further any particular political, organizational, or commercial agenda. In the digital marketplace, the owners of a website that includes paid advertisements stand to receive a small sum every time someone clicks to one of their pages. Neither the reason why a visitor lands on a web page nor the content of a web page matters to the advertiser who is making the payment—the entire financial transaction is entirely based on the number of visitors. Although each payment is small, total payments can add up to large sums. This is where fake news enters the financial picture.

In August 2016 the *Guardian* reported that teenagers in the small town of Veles, Macedonia, were running over 150 websites featuring mostly pro–Donald Trump fake new articles. Rather than having any politically motivated interest in the US elections, the owners of these websites were creating fake news stories as a way to earn money. The websites featured pro-Trump articles simply because these generated more income than pro-Clinton articles.[3] Similarly, in March 2017, *60 Minutes* reported on a American purveyor of fake news who claimed to have no political motivations yet was earning $10,000 a month from advertising revenues generated by such fabricated stories as a report that the US Army had quarantined an entire Texas town due to an Ebola outbreak and another claiming that anyone who signs up for Obamacare would be implanted with a RFID tracking chip.[4] Claims of nonpartisan intent by the creators of mercenary fake news aside, the effect of their fake news articles can be identical to that of propaganda pieces.

Clickbait articles, which use alluring, often sensationalistic headlines to attract readers, can be considered a form a mercenary fake news, especially when the connection between the headlines and the actual content of the article is tenuous.

Fake News with an Agenda

When fake news is intentionally created to promote a specific agenda, it becomes part of the subset of the fake news called *propaganda*. There are any number of websites and online commentators who deal entirely or largely in propagandistic fake news, though few would openly admit to being a propagandist.

Satirical Fake News

An entirely different genre of fake news consists of satirical stories created for purposes of humor as well as, in many cases, political or social commentary. Jonathan Swift's famous satirical essay "A Modest Proposal" is darkly humorous due to the preposterous nature of the barbaric "solution" (i.e., eating infants) it offers for reducing poverty in Ireland, yet, at the same time, the essay serves as a critical commentary on both the political situation in Ireland and the then-common practice of pamphleteers offering up impractical, half-baked solutions to complex problems. The long-running web publication *The Onion* is perhaps the leading US source of satirical fake news stories, though it is certainly not the only such source. Taken out of context, satirical stories can be mistaken for serious news and opinion. For just one of many recent examples, in March 2017 several Chinese publications reported as serious news a satirical story about President Donald Trump that was originally published as humor in the *New Yorker*.[5]

PROPAGANDA AS A SUBSET OF FAKE NEWS

Propaganda is a subset of fake news that is typically used to further a political agenda, though it also may be used to further nonpolitical agendas. The word *propaganda* is so loaded with negative connotations that labeling any information as propaganda is to characterize it as both a lie and inherently malevolent. Few creators of information ever want to hear their handiwork labeled as propaganda. However, propaganda does not necessarily serve an ill purpose. During World War II, the Allies constantly churned out propaganda as part of the effort to defeat the Axis Powers, something most people would consider to be at least a legitimate (if not a straight-up virtuous) use of propaganda. Similarly, while public service announcements against social ills like drunk driving or bullying may be quite propagandistic, their intention is to further a worthwhile cause.

Propaganda is not a new phenomenon, having been around for a couple of millennia now. The oldest example of written propaganda is a description of the conquests of Darius the Great dating from circa 515 BCE. Since that time, the world has endured an almost constant stream of propaganda generated by societies as diverse as Ancient Rome, the Qing Dynasty, and (perhaps most notoriously) Nazi Germany. In the present day, any number of countries employ propaganda on a regular basis, with North Korea standing out as a leading contemporary example of a propaganda state. That said, propaganda is not the exclusive property of any one nation, creed, or political party—the backers of just about every cause have employed propaganda at one time or another to exaggerate the greatness of their cause, denigrate the other side, or, most commonly, do both. Propaganda is often divided into three types:

1. *White propaganda:* the propagandist openly acknowledges authorship of the propaganda.
2. *Gray propaganda:* the authorship of the propaganda is left ambiguous.
3. *Black propaganda:* the author of the propaganda falsely attributes authorship to an opponent.

Propaganda does not necessarily have to originate from a government or other organization. Private individuals with no official connection to any government or organization can serve as propagandists. For a notorious example of the latter, in 1933 Walter Duranty, then the Moscow correspondent for the *New York Times*, filed stories from the Soviet Union downplaying the severity of a devastating famine that was at the time raging with particular severity in the Ukraine, where millions would perish from starvation and related diseases by the time the famine had run its course. Though Duranty's stories proved to be effective propaganda for dictator Josef Stalin and the Soviet government, Duranty was neither part of that government nor on their payroll. In a 1990 *New York Times* opinion piece which labels Duranty's reports on the famine as "some of the worst reporting to appear in this newspaper," Duranty himself is characterized as

> neither Communist nor swayed by Moscow gold. Instead, his failings reflected a more mundane affliction: he succumbed to a thesis. Having bet his reputation on Stalin, he strove to preserve it by ignoring or excusing Stalin's crimes. He saw what he wanted to see.[6]

Whether you consider Duranty to be an arch villain or a supreme fool, his fixation on seeing only what he wanted to see—in spite of the very strong evidence to the contrary—is an all-too-common human failing. At one time or another, most of us fall into the same trap into which Duranty fell: our filters prevent us from taking in information that contradicts our biases. The difference is that the average person's brushes with shortsightedness and wishful thinking do not, typically, contribute to the deaths of millions or end up in the history books.

Whatever its source of origin, most propaganda mixes a small amount of fact with a large dose of fiction. One notorious piece of propaganda which Adolf Hitler's Nazi Party was particularly fond of promoting centered on the so-called stab-in-the-back myth. According to the stab-in-the-back myth, the German Army of World War I was never defeated in the field but was, instead, betrayed—stabbed in the back—by the traitorous "November criminals" who signed the armistice on November 11, 1918. In the eyes of the Nazis, the November criminals were part and parcel of the Nazi Party's traditional scapegoats: Bolsheviks, the various supporters of the interwar Weimar

Republic, and, especially, Jews. There was a tiny bit of truth to the Nazis' stab-in-the-back myth in that, by 1918, large segments of the German population were no longer supportive of the war effort and just wanted the fighting to end. As the privations caused by the war worsened, Germany experienced antiwar strikes by industrial workers as well as a major antiwar mutiny among German Navy personnel that began in early November 1918. However, the bulk of the stab-in-the-back myth was a complete, self-serving fabrication—especially the contention that the German Army was never defeated in the field. After overextending itself in the spring of 1918, the German Army was collapsing under the weight of the combined armies of France, Britain, and the United States and had no chance of winning the war by the time the armistice was signed. It was also a lie that the Nazis' scapegoats were to blame for Germany's defeat. The truth is that one hundred thousand Jewish soldiers fought for Germany in World War I, with twelve thousand of that number dying on the battlefield.[7]

Because what deserves to be labeled as propaganda is highly subjective, it is no surprise that one person's propaganda may be another person's truth. A typical supporter of Adolf Hitler would have no more considered the poster shown in figure 2.2 to be propaganda than a typical American of 1944 would have considered comic books featuring Captain America to be propaganda.

Propaganda, Public Relations, and Advertising

Although propaganda is most closely associated with political aims, its definition can be expanded to include such nonpolitical activities as public relations and advertising.

Public Relations

Such organizations as private-sector businesses, government agencies, and schools pay public relations specialists to enhance their image in the eyes of the public. When things go especially wrong—a company is accused of selling a dangerous product or an agency is called out for mismanagement—public relations staff can turn to propaganda in order to fight back against the resultant negative publicity. In the wake of a shocking sex-abuse scandal that broke in November 2011, Penn State University contracted with the world's largest public relations firm in the hopes of rebuilding the university's severely tarnished image. One week after the contract was signed, a media consultant

FIGURE 2.2

A typical example of Nazi propaganda, this poster glorifies militarism, nationalism, and sacrifice. The text translates as "We will create the new Germany. Think of the sacrifices—elect National Socialists." *Library of Congress*

with connections to the head of Penn State's new public relations firm published an opinion piece in *USA Today* entitled "Penn State Deserves Great Praise." As the title suggests, the author effusively cheers Penn State's efforts to recover from the scandal.[8] It does not require a great deal of skepticism to conclude that this ostensibly impartial opinion piece crosses the border between public relations and propaganda.

Advertising

Commercial advertising is another form of information that might be considered propaganda. There is no arguing that one hallmark of propaganda—mixing a little truth with a lot of fabrication—is also a hallmark of commercial advertising. Brand X may be offering up a bit of truth when it claims nine out of ten doctors recommend it over brand Y, but what brand X's advertisement fails to point out is that a total of only ten handpicked, well-compensated doctors were surveyed while thousands of doctors brand X did not contact would never in a million years recommend its product.

The tobacco industry is especially notorious for its relentless, decades-long campaign to promote cigarette smoking through advertising. Cigarettes have been advertised through every conceivable medium, including billboards, newspapers, magazines, radio, film, television, sports sponsorships, and the Internet. Throughout the twentieth century, cigarette advertisements were such an important source of income for US magazines that only a handful—including *Reader's Digest*, the *New Yorker*, *National Geographic*, *Good Housekeeping*, and *Washington Monthly*—refused to run cigarette advertisements. The fascinating online exhibit "Not a Cough in a Carload" documents how magazine advertisements for cigarettes employed images of doctors, sports figures, celebrities, athletes, and even babies to promote cigarette smoking as glamorous, socially acceptable, and safe.[9] Until television commercials for cigarettes were banned (starting in 1971 in the United States), they played a significant role in popular culture. In the 1960s even small children were familiar with the theme music and catchphrases of cigarette television advertisements. Lark cigarettes used as its theme music "The William Tell Overture," which any self-respecting child of midcentury America would have identified as "the Lone Ranger song." Marlboro television ads used the rousing theme from the popular western film *The Magnificent Seven*. Familiar cigarette catchphrases heard in countless television commercials included the following:

"Winston tastes good, like a cigarette should."

"I'd walk a mile for a Camel."

"Tareyton. I'd rather fight than switch."

Cigarettes were openly advertised on television programs that appealed to the young, including *The Beverly Hillbillies* and *The Flintstones,* both of which featured "cast ads" promoting cigarettes.[10]

After being banned from advertising on US television, cigarette companies responded by expanding their sponsorship of sporting events. From 1972 to 2003, NASCAR's premier racing series was sponsored by the R.J. Reynolds tobacco company and promoted as the Winston Cup. Cigarette companies also resorted to product placement in films to promote smoking in general and their brands in particular. A study of the top twenty-five US films released from 1988 to 1997 (250 films in all) found that tobacco appeared in 80 percent of these films and identifiable tobacco brands appeared in 28 percent of them.[11]

Did all that advertising of cigarettes work? The consensus among scholars who study the relationship between cigarette smoking and advertising is that there is a causal relationship between the two.[12] Does the tobacco industry's collective efforts to promote cigarette smoking equate to a propaganda campaign? While there may be strong feelings about what the answer to this question *should* be, the answer is subjective and it is ultimately up to the individual to decide when advertising becomes propaganda.

Of course, cigarettes are not the only products that use advertising. Even though we like to think we are above its influence, advertising has the potential to shape many of our decisions: the food we eat, the cars we drive, the teams we root for, and the politicians who get our votes. In the end, the power of advertising to shape our decision making is unaffected by whether we choose to label it as propaganda.

WHAT CAN HARRY POTTER TEACH US ABOUT FAKE NEWS AND THE MEDIA?

The books that make up the Harry Potter series are deeply rooted in fantasy, yet, like most fantasies, the series uses imaginary worlds and characters to hold up a mirror to the real world inhabited by real people. One of the real-world phenomena reflected in the mirror of the Harry Potter series is the disruption digital technology was bringing to traditional media at the time J. K. Rowling was writing the books that would make her one of the world's most well-known and wealthy media celebrities.

For a work of fantasy, the Harry Potter series is unusual in that it is set in a clearly identified, real-world location (the United Kingdom) and adheres to a contemporary, real-world time line so specific that it is possible to pinpoint the dates of many events within the series. Harry Potter was born on July 31, 1980, and started his first year at Hogwarts School in early September 1991. Harry, Ron, and Hermione set out on their final quest to find and destroy the evil Voldemort's horcruxes in August 1997, within a few weeks, as it happens, of the real-world death of Diana, Princess of Wales. While this synchronicity may be just a coincidence, it turns out that aspects of the popular reaction to Diana's death resonate in the Harry Potter series.

Traditional media were widely vilified at the time of Diana's death, with the public at large blaming paparazzi as the proximate cause of the princess's fatal accident and accusing magazines, newspapers, and television of indulging in a ratings-fueled, post-tragedy feeding frenzy. The Harry Potter series shares a similarly critical view of traditional media, with the harshness of the criticism increasing in the novels written after Diana's death. In the wizard society to which young Harry Potter is introduced in the first book of the series, the leading newspaper is the *Daily Prophet*. (The pun on *prophet/profit* is clearly intended.) Early on the *Daily Prophet* is portrayed as a rather benign news outlet, but by the middle books of the series it has evolved to become a hurtful scandal sheet as well as a major source of disinformation. Among its sins, the *Daily Prophet* is the employer of Rita Skeeter, an unscrupulous practitioner of yellow journalism whose deceptive articles expose Harry to public ridicule and whose innuendo-filled biography heaps dirt on Headmaster Albus Dumbledore.

By the final volume of the series, the *Daily Prophet* has completely transformed into a dangerous outlet for government propaganda, churning out a constant stream of fake news in order to keep the population in the dark about Voldemort's evil plans to take over the wizarding world and purge it of all who are not pure-blood wizards. Whether or not one believes what is printed in the *Daily Prophet* becomes a litmus test within the wizarding community, inflaming passions and polarizing wizards into antagonistic camps in much the same way that highly partisan digital information has been accused of polarizing people in the real world.

Besides vilifying the *Daily Prophet*, Rowling also takes a few shots at the *Quibbler*, a low-circulation magazine that, when first introduced, specializes in printing unsubstantiated articles supporting crackpot conspiracy theories or proving (unconvincingly) the existence of imaginary creatures (such as the crumpled-horn snorkack) too unbelievable even for a fictional universe in which dragons and hippogriffs are common. However, as the *Daily Prophet* becomes increasingly propagandistic, the *Quibbler*'s publication of articles in support of Harry cast it in a better light.

In addition to generating widespread anger toward traditional media, the international shock over Diana's death spurred people to turn en masse to the web, both as a source of information and as an outlet for expressing opinions and venting emotions. A signal event in the history of the web, Diana's death demonstrated to millions that the old gatekeepers of information—newspapers and television networks—no longer held an absolute monopoly on what could be reported and the ways in which information could be shared. The unprecedented outpouring of user-generated web content relating to the recently deceased Diana was a wake-up call to traditional media. Whereas prior to Diana's death many major print and broadcast media outlets had either ignored the web or merely dabbled in it, after her death both print and broadcast media scrambled to get on the web in a big way. Notably, in September 1997 the BBC hastily launched a temporary website devoted to the events surrounding Diana's death, soon following this up with the establishment of a permanent, full-service BBC web presence in November 1997.[13]

As the web matured and attracted ever more users, it increasingly became the go-to place for nontraditional, alternative media, inspiring in many a hope (which may have been naive) that the web would eventually give rise to a truly free, grassroots media uninfluenced by market forces on one hand and government control on the other. In *The Deathly Hallows*, the final novel in the Harry Potter series, Rowling introduces such a true grassroots media in the form of Potterwatch. With Voldemort's puppet government in complete control of not only the *Daily Prophet*, but also all other mainstream forms of magical communication, a group of rebellious wizards launches Potterwatch as a platform for sharing uncensored, factual news. While the radio-based Potterwatch may be seen as a throwback to the resistance movements that sprang up in Nazi-occupied Europe during World War II, the irreverent, amateurish tone of Potterwatch certainly owes something to the popular image of the late 1990s/early 2000s web as an innovative, upstart, self-governing alternative to the kind traditional media represented by the mainstream *Daily Prophet* and the off-kilter, but still solidly old-school, *Quibbler*. What does not explicitly appear in the Harry Potter series is the emergence of any sort of grassroots (or even pseudo-grassroots) pro-Voldemort counterpoint to Potterwatch. The existence today of thousands of highly partisan information sources on the web suggests that the proliferation of pro-Voldemort echo chambers to counter, and possibly drown out, Potterwatch would have been inevitable.

THE HISTORY OF FAKE NEWS

One thing that can be said with certainty about fake news is that it is hardly a new phenomenon. If we accept that propaganda is a subset of fake news, then we already know that fake news in the form of propaganda dates back more than two thousand years. Even if we don't bring propaganda into the fake news fold, non-propagandistic fake news has been around since long before the start of the Digital Age. One example of fake news from the nineteenth century is the series of non-propagandistic fake news stories published in 1835 by the *New York Sun*. Now known as the Moon Hoax, this series of articles reported in depth on the discovery of life and civilization on the Moon.[14] Besides reporting totally fake news, the author of the Moon Hoax series falsely cites Sir John Herschel, one of the most credible astronomers of the day, as his source of information.

Similarly, on April 13, 1844, the self-same *New York Sun* ran a major story under the following multipart headline rendered in typically ornate nineteenth-century display typeface:

ASTOUNDING
NEWS!
BY EXPRESS VIA NORFOLK!

————————

THE
ATLANTIC CROSSED
IN
THREE DAYS!

————————

SIGNAL TRIUMPH
OF
MR. MONCK MASON'S
FLYING
MACHINE!!!

————————

Arrival at Sullivan's Island, near Charlestown, S. C., of Mr. Mason, Mr.
Robert Holland, Mr. Henson, Mr. Harrison Ainsworth, and four others, in
the
STEERING BALLOON
"VICTORIA,"

AFTER A PASSAGE OF
SEVENTY-FIVE HOURS
FROM LAND TO LAND.

————————

FULL PARTICULARS
OF THE
VOYAGE!!!

Now known as the Balloon Hoax, the story was nothing more than fake
news invented out of whole cloth to sell newspapers to gullible readers. Neither hoax—moon or balloon—was all that unusual for newspapers of the
day. In fact, fake news stories were common enough that the most notable
thing about the Balloon Hoax is the identity of its author, American literary
giant Edgar Allan Poe. Because Poe wrote the Balloon Hoax article strictly for
money—he certainly did not write it to further the agendas of Big Balloon
or the Aeronaut Party—it can be considered an example of mercenary fake
news.

Fake news about moons and balloons did little harm and likely provided
enough amusement to be worth the price of a newspaper. Other fake news
stories were less benign. Fake news stories helped inflame the political passions that led to the US Civil War and served to keep those passions boiling
during the years of conflict. Following the war, the United States entered into
a heyday for fake news that was capped by the yellow journalism of the nineteenth century's final decade. Unburdened by any journalistic standards or
interest in the truth, yellow journalism was all about creating sensationalistic
stories that sold newspapers and brought in advertising dollars (see, for example, figure 2.3). Yellow journalism was responsible (if not entirely, then at
least in part) for starting the Spanish-American War through the publication
of sensationalistic fake news stories blaming fictional atrocities on Spanish
authorities and generally whipping up war fever.

The steady professionalization of journalism over the course of the twentieth century helped to drive fake news out of mainstream media. With, of
course, some exceptions. One remarkable example of a fake news story that
did make it into mainstream media is "Jimmy's World," an article that appeared on the front page of the *Washington Post* on September 28, 1980.
Purporting to tell the story of an eight-year-old heroin addict, "Jimmy's

THE FIN DE SIÈCLE NEWSPAPER PROPRIETOR
He Combines High-Sounding Professions and High-Spiced Sensations, and Reaps a Golden Profit Thereby

FIGURE 2.3
In this 1894 illustration by Frederick Burr Opper entitled "The Fin De Siècle Newspaper Proprietor: He Combines High-Sounding Professions and High-Spiced Sensations, and Reaps a Golden Profit Thereby," the figure outlined in a box in the upper-left corner carries a sheet of paper that reads, "Fake News." *Library of Congress*

World" earned a Pulitzer Prize for its author. When the story was proven to be fictional, the author resigned from the *Washington Post* and returned the Pulitzer Prize.[15] Outside of occasional fake news stories that slipped into mainstream publications, supermarket tabloids became a major source of fake news beginning in the 1950s and continuing into the present day. One such tabloid, the now-defunct *Weekly World News*, was best known for its sensationalistic black-and-white covers and patently fake news stories on such unlikely phenomena as cryptids, aliens, and dead celebrities (especially Elvis Presley) spotted alive and well.

Of course, it was the advent of digital technology—particularly the spread of the web from a playground for computer buffs into something approaching a household necessity—that really allowed fake news to take off. With no standards for accuracy, no way of vetting the qualifications of information creators or the truthfulness of what they created, and almost no way for the libeled to take legal action against their libelers, the web made it possible for anyone to assert just about anything, no facts or credible evidence required. More importantly, the technology of the web made possible the potential for any given piece of information—no matter how false or potentially harmful—to reach millions at virtually no cost. Adding fuel to the fire, the technology of mobile devices eventually made it possible to create, receive, and forward information—credible or not—without even the need to sit down at a computer. Fake news never had it so good.

IS THE FUROR OVER FAKE NEWS YET ANOTHER MORAL PANIC?

With all the attention paid to the fake news phenomenon—especially the gloomy predictions that the world may be heading into some kind of post-truth dark ages in which science, reason, and facts no longer matter—it is worth asking if all the hand-wringing is no more than another moral panic that will soon burn out and be remembered, if at all, with embarrassment and, possibly, shame?

As pointed out several times in this chapter, neither fake news nor propaganda are new phenomena. And even though the harm caused by propaganda has at times in history been devastating (as happened in Nazi Germany), free and democratic societies generally right themselves before allowing propaganda to take them completely over the edge. The existence of propaganda, though a risk, does not necessarily spell doom for society.

Similarly, while people can, and often do, debate the role of fake news in increasing the polarization of society, the existence of a polarized society itself is nothing new. Looking at the history of the United States, events like the Revolutionary War and the Civil War were more than polarizing disagreements—they were bloody conflicts that divided society into armed camps. Literally. Until the attack on Pearl Harbor, the United States was quite polarized when it came to whether the country should get involved in World War II. In the 1960s the Vietnam War sharply divided the country into pro- and antiwar camps that clashed violently on a number of occasions. It is possible that fake news has made societal splits worse, but that thesis is yet to be conclusively proven. It may be that fake news, along with other forms of digital information, has done nothing more than make it harder to ignore how divided people have almost always been. "Harder to ignore" is not, of course, the same thing as "caused."

Another angle to the furor over fake news is that new forms of media, or even just new twists on old media, tend to generate a great deal of anxiety. The world has seen moral panics over (mostly imaginary) dangers posed by theater, radio, movies, music, and television. In the 1950s the United States went into such a moral panic over comic books that comic book publishers voluntarily established the Comics Code Authority, an act of draconian self-regulation publishers took out of the fear that, without the code, the United States government would step in to censor and regulate comic books.[16] When the web was still a novelty, it was quite common for traditional media, especially movies and television, to cast the web as a villain—if for no other reason than the web was drawing viewers away from the very media that was, conveniently, villainizing the web. For one of many possible examples from the early years of the web, in October 1995 the television series *Homicide: Life on the Street* featured an episode entitled "Fire: Part 1." In the episode homicide detectives are investigating the death of a homeless man killed in a building fire. The arson investigator who is assisting the detectives informs them that the fire was an arson and goes on to describe in exact detail the method used to commit the crime. When the detectives ask where anyone would learn the particular method of committing arson just described, the arson investigator replies, with sharp anger and contempt, "the Internet." The detectives shake their heads. Of course, the writers of that episode managed to pull off a neat trick. On one hand, they sanctimoniously blamed the Internet for spreading potentially deadly instructions on how to commit arson; on the other hand, they, through the character of the arson investigator, shared with a television audience numbering in the millions potentially deadly instructions on how to commit arson. (Instructions I won't repeat here because I'm not irresponsible. Also, before I was a librarian I worked as a firefighter.)

Perhaps the most important question to ask about fake news and other forms of noncredible information in digital formats is, "Are people actually falling for this nonsense?" Maybe not as much as we might think. Researchers who studied the impact of fake news and social media on voting in the 2016 US presidential election concluded (with multiple caveats and conditions) that fake news "would have changed vote shares by an amount on the order of hundredths of a percentage point. This is much smaller than Trump's margin of victory in the pivotal states on which the outcome depended."[17] At least in the eyes of these researchers, fake news did not change the outcome of the

HOW FAKE NEWS SET OFF THE SILLIEST MORAL PANIC OF THE TWENTIETH CENTURY

Not all moral panics produce dire outcomes. Sometimes they are the result of mostly harmless hoaxes intentionally created to take in the gullible.

The 1960s were a time of great social upheaval, and one of the biggest concerns of the decade was the increasing use of recreational drugs by young people. Playing on mainstream fears about drug use—at least some of which were overhyped and overheated—the counterculture newspaper the *Berkeley Barb* published in 1967 a bit of fake news in the form of a made-up recipe for extracting from banana peels a psychoactive substance the writers dubbed "bananadine."[18]

Of course, there is no such substance as bananadine nor is it possible to get high from banana peels. Even so, the story spread, with members of the hippie counterculture playing along by claiming to get high from banana peels and sometimes displaying banana peels in public to disturb and provoke the establishment squares. The banana peel story was taken seriously enough that major newspapers began reporting on this new form of drug use that, unlike marijuana and LSD, would be virtually impossible to criminalize. Even the normally staid *Wall Street Journal* ran an article with the headline "Light Up a Banana: Students Bake Peels to Kick Up Their Heels: Exhilarating Effect Is Gained by Legal Puffing, Some Say."[19]

The great bananadine panic of 1967 soon blew over and is mostly forgotten today. As moral panics go, this one was not so bad. Nobody got hurt or sent to prison, and sales of bananas enjoyed a temporary surge.

2016 election, like it or not. Along similar lines, a researcher of media literacy who studied Internet users from multiple countries found that most used search engines to find news rather than going to partisan websites or hiding out in bias-confirming echo chambers. In the words of this researcher, the "panic over fake news, echo chambers and filter bubbles is exaggerated, and not supported by the evidence from users across seven countries."[20] Because the research into fake news is still in its infancy, future researchers are likely to report different, possibly contradictory, findings on just how readily people swallow the bait of fake news.

Whether the furor over the fake news phenomenon is a moral panic has yet to be determined. It took a good decade for the late-1980s and early-1990s fears about ritual Satanic abuse to be exposed as an unfounded moral panic.[21] Sadly, that exposure came too late for the many innocent people who had to endure costly and embarrassing court trials and, in some cases, spend years in jail for made-up crimes they never committed. What is undeniable is that fake news, propaganda, and other misleading forms of information really exist and that their existence demands we carefully evaluate the credibility of the information we encounter.

WHAT IS NEW ABOUT THE FAKE NEWS PHENOMENON

Given that both fake news and propaganda have existed for years, is there anything new about fake news in the Digital Age? Yes, a few things are new. And the thread connecting these new things is digital technology itself.

Information Overload

By the middle of 2017 the total number of web pages numbered around 4.48 billion, a bit more than half a web page for every person on the planet.[22] The number of Twitter accounts had reached 328 million.[23] And the number of monthly Facebook users stood at 1.9 billion.[24] While there are many more numbers that could be added to this roll call of mind-boggling statistics, the point is clear: by any measure—number of web pages, tweets, books, journal articles, images, videos, emails, bytes—the amount of information available in the Digital Age is beyond human comprehension.

Just consider how much less access to information people had in the not-so-distant past. Even after the development of printing from moveable type in the middle of the fifteenth century, books remained expensive and relatively rare. For most of history libraries were tiny compared to what is available from even a modest modern public or academic library (not to mention what is available via the web). It is sobering to consider that many of the greatest thinkers of the printed-book era never set foot in a library—or any other building—that contained more than a few thousand books. In the time of Isaac Newton, the library of his Cambridge University college (Trinity) held from 3,000 to 4,000 volumes; at the time of Newton's death, his personal library, which was large for the time, consisted of some 2,100 volumes.[25] Jumping forward in time, in the mid-nineteenth-century United States a total of 126 college libraries held, in aggregate, just under 600,000 volumes, nearly 120,000 of which were the property of three libraries: Princeton, Yale, and Harvard.[26] It was not until the twentieth century that the book collections of any save the largest academic libraries began approaching sizes that would be considered even midlevel by the standards of today. The University of Illinois, for one example, grew from 66,639 volumes in 1904 to 440,372 volumes in 1920, at which point it had bragging rights as the ninth largest (measured by number of volumes) academic library in the United States.[27] By way of comparison, in 2017 the combined libraries of the ten University of California campuses held some 39 million print volumes along with vast amounts of content in digital formats.[28]

Because no previous generation has had to contend with so much information or had such easy access to information, no previous generation has suffered so much from information overload—the inability to grasp a concept or make a decision because there is simply too much information to process. A number of causes contribute to information overload:

- The amount of information and the speed at which it is created
- The number of channels through which information can be communicated (Twitter, Instagram, Facebook, YouTube, television, newspapers, etc.)
- The ease with which information can be duplicated and forwarded
- Contradictory information (as when economic statistics contradict each other)
- Information lacking credibility (fake news, propaganda, partisan spin)
- Information lacking context (as when bits of information are cherry-picked and the identity of the original source is absent)
- The challenges of determining what information is credible and what is not

With so much information and so much uncertainty over what information to trust and what to dismiss, individuals may respond by resorting to
coping mechanisms. One way of coping with information overload is to tune
out, to simply stop paying attention to information: "Instead of trying to
understand climate change, I'm going to watch cat videos." Another coping
mechanism is to limit information intake to a few trusted sources and, in the
worst case, to trust those sources without question. This leads to the informa-
tion-bubble phenomenon in which individuals take in only information that
reaffirms their existing social and political biases. Whatever the causes and
whatever the coping mechanisms, information overload is an aspect of the
fake news phenomenon that is much newer than fake news itself.

Reaching a Large Audience at a Low Cost

Imagine the following scenario. The year is 1989 and you are a member of
a small but dedicated group of Kennedy-assassination conspiracy buffs trying to publicize a theory about the assassination that is considered too weird,
fringe, extreme, or flat-out crazy to get any traction in mainstream media.
Since this is the pre-web era, you employ a typewriter or a word processor to
create a five-page manifesto promoting your group's agenda. You take a copy
of your manifesto to a photocopy center and pay to have one thousand copies
made (5 pages x .03 per page x 1,000 copies = $150). You then distribute cop-
ies of your manifesto either by hand or through the mail. Let's say you really
luck out and, on average, every single copy is read by three different readers.
Congratulations! An audience of three thousand is now aware of your theory
that the assassination of President Kennedy was masterminded by textbook
publishers. (The evidence is all there. Oswald worked in the Texas *School
Book* Depository. Wake up, sheeple!) And all it cost you to reach three thousand readers was $150 dollars, plus your time, plus whatever you spent on
delivery and/or postage. (That cost is in 1989 dollars, when the US federal
minimum wage was $3.35 per hour.)

In the Digital Age, tallying up three thousand likes on a Facebook post,
while decent, is hardly considered blowing up the Net. Not when an item that
goes full-on viral will rack up views numbering in the millions. Millions of
views, yet it costs almost nothing to create and distribute that piece of digital
information via the Internet. Unlike the situation in 1989, when the cost of
copying and distribution would serve as a check on the number of times any

individual or group could afford to make and distribute multiple copies of paper documents, in the online world anyone can create and distribute digital content at almost no marginal cost. Not every piece of digital content is going to go viral, of course, but it only takes one success to get a message in front of millions of people. A dedicated individual or group can, at very low cost, crank out tweets, Facebook posts, and fake news stories again and again and again in the hopes that one of those items will connect with a large audience. The potential to reach a very large audience at a very low cost is something that simply was not possible prior to the Digital Age.

Ease of Alteration

A third difference between information in the Digital Age and information in earlier times is the ease with which digital information can be altered. While fakes and forgeries existed prior to digital technology, altering a physical object such as a paper document or a photographic print was not particularly easy or common. In 1920, a series of five photographs purporting to prove the existence of fairies generated a great deal of interest in the United Kingdom and abroad (see figure 2.4).

While the photograph in figure 2.4 leaps out as a crude fake by the image standards of the twenty-first century, altered photographs were enough of a rarity in the early twentieth century that some, including Sir Arthur Conan Doyle, the creator of Sherlock Holmes, believed the Cottingley fairies photographs to be genuine.

Today the technology for altering documents, images, sounds, and video is not only much better than what was available just a few years ago, it is also more prevalent and much easier to use. Altered photographs show up on the Internet all the time. Sometimes the purpose of such photographs is benign, perhaps to entertain or amuse, but altered photographs can also be used to mislead. In 2004, opponents of presidential candidate John Kerry distributed a convincing photograph showing him at a 1971 antiwar rally seated next to controversial actress Jane Fonda. The photograph showing Kerry and Fonda together turned out to be a faked compilation of two photographs taken at different times and locations.[29] Like a lot of propaganda, the altered photo mixed truth with fiction. That both Kerry (a decorated Vietnam veteran) and Fonda had attended antiwar rallies in the early 1970s was true. That they had attended the same rally and sat together was false.

FIGURE 2.4
Altered photograph depicting a young woman with one of the Cottingley fairies. *Elsie Wright and Frances Griffiths*

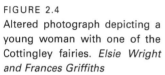

Digital technology facilitates the altering of not just still images but of audio and video as well. The 2016 film *Rogue One: A Star Wars Story* famously used CGI (computer-generated imagery) to make it seem that actress Carrie Fisher appeared in the film as a youthful Princess Leia when, at the time *Rogue One* was shot, Fisher was sixty years old and would, to the dismay of fans, pass away shortly after the film's premiere. In the same year that *Rogue One* premiered, Adobe Systems introduced VoCo, a new technology that has been described as "Photoshop for audio." With VoCO technology and twenty minutes of any individual's recorded voice, editing speech becomes as simple as editing text in a word processing document.[30] It is easy to imagine many ways this technology could be used to create deceptive information. For example, how easy would it be for someone equipped with VoCo and access to historic audio recordings to create, say, a convincing recording of Lyndon Baines Johnson admitting in his own voice that he (in collusion, of course, with textbook publishers) was personally responsible for the assassination of John F.

Kennedy? More realistically, how easy would it be for a political operative to create an audio file of a political opponent saying something so offensive that it could change the outcome of an election? For police to create an audio file of a suspect "confessing" to a crime in his or her own voice?

Other Tricky Technologies

Besides making it easier to create misleading information, digital technology has other tricks it can play on anyone attempting to evaluate the credibility of information.

Political Bots

Political bots are automated computer programs that use algorithms to generate political messages. While some political bots acknowledge up front that their messages are machine generated, some deceptively present their messages as human generated. According to a trio of computer scientists affiliated with Oxford University's Project on Computation Propaganda,

> Political actors and governments worldwide have begun using bots to manipulate public opinion, choke off debate, and muddy political issues. Political bots tend to be developed and deployed in sensitive political moments when public opinion is polarized.[31]

These same computer scientists estimated that at certain key times during the 2016 US presidential elections up to a one-third of all political tweets promoting Donald Trump were machine generated.[32] That said, it is important to note that the Hillary Clinton campaign also used political bots. But rather than focusing on which candidate is the bigger cheater, the focus should be on the fact that everyone needs to be aware that messages appearing to be from other human beings may be machine generated. There are a couple of tricks for detecting messages from bots. Political bots send messages around the clock, while humans take time away from posting messages for things like jobs and sleep. Political bots tend to be fixated on a single topic and to repeat the same words, slogans, and catchphrases over and over, while humans tend to send messages about a variety of topics and to vary their use of language. If you are not sure if a tweet is from a human or a bot, the Indiana University–based Botometer can help you decide.[33]

Machine-Written Articles

In much the same vein as political bots that create tweets, software now exists that is capable of writing news articles with a minimum of human input. Both the Associated Press and Fox News make limited use of machine-written articles, and software for generating machine-written articles is now freely available to the public.[34] While machine-written articles are, thus far, a rarity, they are yet another factor to consider when evaluating information.

Search Engine Optimization

Search engines like Google and Bing use algorithms to produce naturally ranked (i.e., not influenced by payment or human biases) search results. Search engine algorithms consider a number of factors when ranking results, such as the frequency with which the search term appears on a site, the number of links made to a site, a site's overall popularity, and so on. If you ever wonder why, for example, *Wikipedia* often appears at the top of many search engine results, it is not because *Wikipedia* pays for the privilege; it is because *Wikipedia* pages have earned their high rankings based on the search engine's algorithm.

In a perfect world, search engine rankings would always be impartial and uninfluenced by those who wish to game the system. In the real world, people try to game the system all the time through a process known as search engine optimization (SEO). In its defense, SEO can be used as legitimate marketing practice to boost a website's visibility and drive more visitors to a target website. Businesses and organizations routinely seek to boost their online presence by paying computer experts to provide SEO services. However, so-called black-hat SEO can be used to damage the reputation of individuals, businesses, and organizations; to unnaturally inflate the prominence of selected websites; or to promote specific political or social agendas. Practitioners of black-hat SEO can employ a number of tactics, including "keyword spamming, generating massive numbers of low-quality pages, creating artificial link networks, and creating deceptive web pages that appear differently to users and search engines."[35] Whatever the techniques may be, the takeaway for anyone who uses search engines is to be aware that the search results you see may have been manipulated to produce biased, unnatural, and unearned rankings.

Identifying when search results have been manipulated through SEO is not easy, but it is most likely to occur when searching for information on a politically controversial topic or information about a candidate during a hotly contested election. Here are three signs that search results may have been intentionally manipulated through search engine optimization:

1. The top results all repeat the same partisan message in essentially the same way.
2. The top results consist of a mix of well-known partisan websites along with obscure partisan websites that normally do not rank highly.
3. Less partisan, better known websites do not appear among the top rankings.

Technology being the relentless beast that it is, there is no doubt additional tricky technologies are already out there or will soon emerge, each one capable of deceiving even the most cautious users of information. Nobody said that evaluating information in the Digital Age was going to be easy or that keeping current on the latest tricks and technology for promoting misinformation would not be an ongoing task. Stay alert. Keep your guard up.

RECAP

Fake news is a complex concept with multiple definitions. It is important to understand how the term *fake news* is being used in any given context.

Propaganda is a form of misinformation that is intentionally created to further a specific agenda (political, organizational, or commercial). Propaganda, which has been around for thousands of years, is a subset of fake news.

Fake news includes propaganda, but may also include misinformation created for proposes other than furthering a specific agenda. Fake news has been around for many years, though it exploded into a worldwide media sensation at the end of 2016. For the purposes of this book, fake news can be classified into three main types:

1. *Mercenary fake news:* created for profit with no concern about the content of the message
2. *Fake news with an agenda:* propaganda

3. *Satirical fake news:* created for humorous purposes but may also function
   as political or social commentary and criticism

For all the attention paid to fake news and hand-wringing over its dangers
to democracy, it is fair to ask if all this concern constitutes a moral panic.
Whether fake news, as it exists in the Digital Age, is truly as dangerous as
some believe it to be remains to be seen.

While fake news, including propaganda, is not new, there are a few new
twists to fake news in the Digital Age:

- Information overload makes evaluating information harder than it has ever
  been in the past.
- Digital technology makes it easy to distribute fake news to a potentially
  huge audience at a very low cost.
- Digital technology makes it easy to alter information—including photographs, audio recordings, and video—for the purposes of misleading the
  recipients of that information.

A number of relatively new technologies give purveyors of misinformation
sophisticated tools for carrying out deceptions:

- Political bots produce machine-generated content, such as tweets, that may
  falsely appear to be human-generated content.
- Software makes it possible to create machine-written articles that require
  minimal human input. As with tweets produced by political bots, these
  articles may falsely appear to be generated by humans.
- Search engine optimization can mislead by re-ranking search engine results
  to drive less credible information to the top of a results list while driving
  more credible information to the bottom.

It is inevitable that new deceptive technologies will continue to emerge and
that masters of deception will deploy them. Anyone who uses information
faces the lifelong challenge of staying aware of these technologies and learning how to detect and defeat them.

Tricks of the Trade

Techniques That Lower Your Information Guard

The world is full of information that is not credible. Some of this misinformation is easy to spot. Quite a lot of it is not. If you care about the credibility of the information you use as part of your decision-making processes, it is up to you to perform due diligence before accepting any information as credible. I like to think of this process as keeping up my *information guard* in the face of a flood of information capable of misleading, deceiving, and quite possibly controlling my decisions. The focus of this chapter is all about defense, about learning to recognize the tools and tricks of deception so that you do not get taken in by misinformation.

ALL OF THE PEOPLE SOME OF THE TIME

This is a true story. In November 2007, when my daughter was still in elementary school, I came upon a video demonstrating a really cool phenomenon. The makers of the video mixed hydrogen peroxide and baking soda into a plastic bottle of a certain brand of soft drink.[1] (I won't name the brand, but let's just say it is noted for its high caffeine content, is popular among those who devote serious amounts of time to video games, and goes well with crispy cheese-flavored snacks). When the creators of the video shook up the solution, it produced a powerful, almost magical, green glow. On the way home from work that evening I stopped by the grocery store and bought a bottle of the soft drink used in the video. That night my daughter and I carefully

NO PATENT ON DECEPTION

This chapter will go into detail on common techniques used to pass off deceptive information as credible. As you learn about these techniques, it is important to remember that nobody has the patent on deception. Just as those you disagree with or, quite possibly, despise will practice deceptive techniques to advance their cause, so too will those you agree with and greatly admire. Because people are human beings and not AI robots, it is much harder to spot deception when members of "my team" are practicing it as opposed to when those rotten jerks on the other side are up to their usual sneaky tricks. This means that your information guard should actually be higher when you are evaluating information that speaks to your happy place than when you are evaluating information that makes you want to punch a brick wall. This is not an easy thing to do.

On the flip side, there is nothing inherently wrong with information that expresses an opinion, supports a point of view, or puts forward an argument for or against something. Almost all information, and certainly the most interesting sort of information, has a point to make rather than being blandly neutral. What to watch out for, then, is when the information creators' desire to make a point becomes so powerful that they resort to using deceptive techniques.

combined the ingredients as instructed and shook the bottle like our lives depended on it. Nothing. We adjusted the quantities. More frantic shaking. More disappointment. What were we doing wrong?

After a good thirty minutes of fussing, shaking, and growing disappointment, it hit me. No. It couldn't be. I went online and did the fact-checking I should have done from the start. It took me about one minute to determine the video was a big, fat hoax. There was no chemical reaction. The magical light effect came from a glow stick the perpetrators had surreptitiously inserted into the bottle. Ugh! How could I be so gullible?

I mean that literally. How could I? A good part of my professional life has been devoted to preaching the gospel of evaluating information, of not accepting facts or evidence without first checking them out, and yet I was taken in by an obvious hoax that some rube who just fell off the turnip truck from Hokeyville should have seen right through.

The point of my confession is that anyone can be deceived by misinformation, even someone who has a high (in one particular case, far too high) opinion of his ability to smell an informational rat. I was fortunate that the deception cost me nothing more than a bottle of soda pop, a few pennies' worth of household chemicals, and a little bit of pride. People have lost thousands of dollars, even their entire life savings, to Internet scams not much more sophisticated than the glowing-soda-pop video hoax.

So why do people fall for misleading information? I know why I fell for it. I fell because the message of the video—mix together a few ordinary household items to produce something spectacular—appealed to my bias for do-it-yourself homemade fun over prepackaged fun that someone else makes for you. I fell because the video had me anticipating the delight my daughter would express on seeing the solution light up like a potion from *Harry Potter*. (Even more, it had me anticipating how good I—*wonderful father that I am*—would feel for being the one to show my daughter this bit of real-world magic in a bottle.) I fell because the prideful part of my brain had me imagining my genius daughter, upon accepting the Nobel Prize for Advanced Science-olo-graphy, mentioning in her speech how it all started the day her dear old dad brought home a bottle of high-octane soda and mixed in a few items from the kitchen cupboard. That fake video hit a grand slam by simultaneously appealing to my existing biases, my ego, my vanity, and my wishful thinking. Which is to say the video so thoroughly appealed to my emotions that I let down my information guard and ended up getting good and snookered. Sad to say, this can happen to anyone at any time.

EMOTIONS AND YOUR INFORMATION GUARD

Having your emotions appealed to in order to manipulate you, for good or bad, is a universal experience. Children and parents, husbands and wives, brothers and sisters—all manipulate each other's emotions to get what they want from each other. Pets can manipulate your emotions. So can friends and classmates and work colleagues and bosses. Politicians and advertisers do it to gain power and money. It happens in the physical world and it happens online. There is nothing wrong with having emotions, of course. Emotions pretty much go with having a detectable heartbeat. And there need not be anything wrong with doing something because someone played on your emotions. It is OK if I go outside to throw the ball for my dog because she made me feel guilty for ignoring her—though it is important that I be aware of why I am doing it. What you have to watch out for is when your emotions are played on so subtly that you do not realize you are being manipulated.

If you were trying to put together a list of emotions that can be played on to get you to drop your information guard, you could do a lot worse than starting with the following:

Anger: Many fake news stories do a land-office business in anger, in getting your blood boiling so hard that you forget to ask yourself if the outrage being reported is genuine, highly exaggerated, or completely made up (see, for example, figure 3.1). It is especially easy to get angry enough to drop your information guard when it is *those idiots on the other side* who are, as usual, up to no good. The problem with anger, even when it is justified, is that it can cause you to accept as true information that you might question if you were in a calmer state of mind. Also, anger is not a particularly helpful tool for making the best decisions. As the example of road rage proves, anger can be a good alarm, but it is a lousy compass.

Greed: This is the emotion that con artists, digital or otherwise, depend on for separating people (some would say "fools") from their money. The allure of increasing the size of your bankroll is hard for anyone to resist, whether that increase comes from a "surefire system for generating wealth" or "locked-in betting tips for beating the football point spread this very weekend." Of course, if someone has a surefire system or locked-in tips, it is a fair question to ask why they are going through all the time and expense of selling their information to strangers when they could instead use their knowledge to make money without any middleman. And why do the makers of these offers so often urge you to "*Act now!*" rather than suggesting you take the time to evaluate just what it is they are selling? These questions are mysteries of the information world, like why online advertisers who urge you to buy gold

FIGURE 3.1
This famous illustration of the Boston Massacre, which was engraved by Boston silversmith and patriot Paul Revere, is today regarded as a highly sensationalized, biased, and mostly inaccurate depiction of the event. The creators of this illustration twisted the facts in order to provoke feelings of anger among their fellow colonists and, by so doing, win support for the American cause. *Library of Congress*

because "paper money will soon be worthless" are willing to sell you their gold for your (soon-to-be-worthless) paper money. Greed can cause you to overlook the need to evaluate the credibility of any information holding out the tempting promise of a golden opportunity.

Envy: A close cousin of anger, envy is triggered by tales of those who have too much, have it too easy, or simply have more than you do. There is an entire genre of memes called "Rich Kids of the Internet" consisting of photographs allegedly depicting spoiled, hyper-wealthy young people either being shamelessly wasteful or ostentatiously flaunting their wealth. The sight of overprivileged twits pouring expensive champagne over the sides of giant yachts or whining that the Ferrari daddy bought them is the wrong color tends to peg the envy meter at the top of the scale. On the other side of the income divide is information focusing on lazy moochers living quite well off the government dime without doing a day's work. Either way, envy can make you forget to ask whether the information you see before your eyes is credible and actually representative of, respectively, the very rich or the very poor.

Pride: Puffing up someone with flattery is the surest way to trigger this emotion. Who, after all, could be smarter, more right-thinking, or straight-up better than you? Why should you, as decent and right thinking as you are, doubt for one minute any information reconfirming that your biases, hunches, gut feelings, and most cherished beliefs are justified and correct? Why should you—*you*, of all people—question any information that asserts your team, profession, political party, religion, or nationality is more deserving than all the others? Why? Because pats on the back make it difficult to see that you are being flattered into accepting misinformation.

Sloth: What's better than getting something for nothing? Simply reply to a Nigerian prince and wait for all that sweet, sweet oil money to come gushing in. Or pay a small handling fee to receive some great freebie. But bothering to check if the opportunity is genuine or just another scam? That's way too much work.

Lust: As the expression "the world's oldest profession" implies, humans long ago discovered that there is money in lust. The online world is filled with phony—yet apparently profitable—schemes based on false promises to fulfill this most basic of human emotions. If you want examples, you can find them for yourself online. You won't have to look very hard.

Gluttony: Gluttony, in the sense of overconsumption of anything, has been a staple of misleading advertisements for decades. Most would agree that an advertisement normalizing the consumption of a 2,500-calorie meal is, at best, misleading. Really any information that promotes conspicuous consumption—live in a giant, energy-gobbling mansion; own a sports car (heck, make it two or three) that costs more than the average family home; travel the world in a state of luxury that would make Louis XIV blush—counts on human gluttony to stop people from asking if what they are being sold has even the slightest acquaintance with everyday reality.

Some readers may recognize the preceding emotions as corresponding to the seven deadly sins. And so they do. Sin or not, just about any human emotion can be played on to manipulate people into letting down their information guard. While listing every single emotion and how misinformation plays on each would belabor the point beyond endurance, two additional emotions—fear and joy—deserve more discussion because they are so prominent among the emotions played upon by purveyors of misinformation

Fear

One of the most primal emotions to which manipulators can appeal, fear can lead people to do and tolerate things they would never do or tolerate if they were not afraid. Dictators use fear—both fear of the threat posed by *the other* and fear of the dictator's own ruthless methods of control—to subjugate entire nations, to convince people to commit terrible acts and put up with intolerable tyranny and deprivations. Like anger, fear is not the best tool for informing sound decisions, and, again like anger, fear can cause people to readily believe information without taking the steps to make sure it is credible.

History is filled with examples of terrible wrongs committed when false fears are stirred up by deceptive information. The witch hunts of medieval Europe, which resulted in the executions of tens of thousands of innocent people, were set off by propaganda that played on fear. The unlawful internment of people of Japanese descent—many of whom were American citizens—during World War II was brought about by misinformation that played on unfounded fears. As for contemporary instances of fearmongering, it only takes a quick scan of news headlines to identify more examples than anyone would like to acknowledge.

Which is not to say that information that causes you to feel fear is always misinformation. If you are driving along a winding, isolated mountain road and see a makeshift sign that reads, "Danger! Bridge Out! 50 Feet," the information on that sign likely makes you feel fear. And your natural fear reaction—bringing your car to a stop without worrying about whether that information is credible—is the correct and rational thing to do. Assuming the bridge really is out, the fact that the information on the sign caused you to feel fear is negated by the fact that the information very likely saved your life. The problem is when the information playing on fear proves to be false. A prankster repeatedly yelling, "There's a bomb in the stadium!" is dangerous because doing so could set off an unnecessary, possibly deadly panic as people quite logically react to the information without wasting a lot of time to determine if it is true or not.

Barring an emergency situation in which seconds matter, however, it is important to evaluate the credibility of any information that makes you feel afraid, important to remember that the fear you are feeling has lowered your information guard and left you vulnerable to misinformation.

Joy

Even though joy is about as far as you can get from so negative an emotion as fear, it too can be used to lower your information guard. In a world in which bad news seems to be the only constant, who does not want to believe joyful, uplifting stories reporting on good people and good things? But just as people have a propensity to unquestioningly believe information that makes them angry or fearful, they have a propensity to believe information that makes them feel joy, regardless of whether that information is credible.

Who wouldn't feel like a bit of a Grinch for questioning the credibility of a heartwarming story about a brave and adorable child's successful fight against cancer? What kind of killjoy casts doubt on a story about a generous good Samaritan (who, surprise, turns out to be a celebrity admired by millions of fans)? Or dares to question the truth of a satisfying tale in which a likable, unassuming hero quietly, yet publicly, delivers a bit of karmic justice to some stuck-up, entitled, self-important jerk? Who really wants to pooh-pooh a breathless report on some exciting new technology that is going to fix a seemingly insoluble worldwide problem or a miracle cure that promises to eliminate a devastating malady? Even when you are aware that all good news is not credible news, the right piece of fake good news told in the right way can worm its way through your defenses and into your heart.

The online world has spawned a neologism, *glurge*, to describe misinformation that plays on the desire to unquestioningly accept that which makes you happy. Glurge, while superficially being all about goodness and rightness, not only is fake but also carries with it undertones of insincerity, hypocrisy, and moral superiority. (The TV Tropes website provides a lengthy discussion of glurge that includes many excellent examples of the genre.[2]) Glurge or not, if information makes you feel especially joyful or righteous in your thinking, your information guard is probably lower than you realize. This is not to say that information that brings you joy and reaffirms your faith in humanity is

LEAD AND VIOLENCE

I have another true confession to share. Many years ago, I heard someone on a radio interview program state that the long-term drop in violent crime in the United States can be attributed to the elimination of leaded gasoline. Lead from gas fumes, the theory goes, damages the brain in ways that contribute to violent behavior. Simply removing the lead from gasoline (and other products, such as paint) reduces violent behavior.

My instantaneous, emotion-driven reaction was to unquestionably accept this theory as true. Why? Because it punched all my happy buttons to think that steps taken to improve the environment had paid off with a profound and unexpected benefit.

Was I wrong to accept that information as true? Not entirely. While the long-term drop in violent crime in the United States is most likely attributable to multiple causes, it turns out there is some credible evidence that reducing lead in the environment numbers among those causes.[3]

Should I have checked out that information before accepting it? Absolutely. That the information may have some truth to it is a mere coincidence that I only discovered after the fact. The lesson to me is that I need to evaluate information that makes me happy as carefully as I evaluate information that makes me angry or fearful.

always false. Good news can be as credible, or not, as bad news. Just remember when that warm glow of joy kicks in to be sure to check out the facts before breaking into your happy dance.

DECEPTIVE TECHNIQUES AND HOW TO SPOT THEM

The most basic tool of deception is good, old-fashioned lying. People will say and write things that are not true, grossly exaggerated, or only partly true. People will fake documents, photographs, audio, and video to make something that is false appear to be true. And, as described earlier, people will play on your emotions to manipulate you into falling for misinformation. There is no one-size-fits-all means of detecting whether information is credible, but becoming aware of the most common tools of deception can go a long way toward helping you spot misinformation.

Confounding Correlation with Causation

Confounding correlation with causation is a very familiar technique for assigning either credit or blame for a particular outcome. A current example of correlation confounded with causation is the argument that autism is related to childhood immunizations. The correlation is based on the fact that the number of autism diagnoses began to rise as childhood immunizations became more frequent. What is missing, at least as far as medical science is concerned, is a causation—a scientifically verifiable explanation for how immunization increases the occurrence of autism.

Of course, it is theoretically possible that medical science will someday discover a causation that proves correct those who claim immunizations contribute to autism. Until that day, which may never come, the immunization-autism connection is merely a time-based correlation that lacks any causation.

The lack of causation does not stop people from using correlation to support their positions. All it really takes to make a correlation is an understanding of how calendars work:

The American League introduced the Designated Hitter Rule in April 1973. In October of that same year, the OPEC oil embargo caused the price of oil to rise by 400 percent. The Designated Hitter rule caused the oil crisis.

Or, much more likely, the Designated Hitter Rule had nothing at all to do with the oil crisis. For even more, and more entertaining, examples of the misuse of correlations, check out the Spurious Correlations website (www .tylervigen.com/spurious-correlations).

Covering Up with Cleverness

This trick is easy to overlook because things that strike you as funny or clever tend to disarm you. A sharp bit of satire, a clever bumper sticker, a memorable slogan, a meme that makes you laugh out loud—any of these can be used to make a point while making you forget to ask if the information conveyed is credible. Even worse, a spoonful of cleverness can be used to make truly hateful medicine seem palatable. Just look at the thousands of clever and funny (at least to sympathizers) memes inhabiting the online world, some of which advocate truly repellent ideas (see, for example, figure 3.2[4]).

Denouncing Hypocrisy

Denouncing the hypocrisy of those with whom they disagree is practically the go-to strategy for anyone commenting on controversial topics.

> She says that nobody has the right to tell her what she can or cannot do with her body, yet she wants to limit my right to smoke cigarettes and ride my motorbike without a helmet.

> He says he's pro-life, but he is all in favor of the military bombing civilian targets.

The reason it is easy to point out an opponent's hypocrisy is that almost everyone is a hypocrite to one extent or another. In fact, there is a word for people who are so consistent in their beliefs that they cannot be accused of hypocrisy. That word is *fanatic*. Even so, the fact that hypocrisy is nearly universal does not stop people from disliking hypocrites and calling out hypocrisy when they see it.

For example, suppose candidate X vocally supports Libertarian economic principles but is also in favor of government agriculture subsidies. Some voters might decide not to vote for candidate X because they think holding both views is hypocritical and makes candidate X unworthy of their trust. But even

MOVE ON, MAROON BROTHER, MOVE ON!

FIGURE 3.2
Originally published in 1894 as a work of humor, *Bill Nye's History of the United States* includes this illustration by comic artist Frederick Burr Opper. Although the intent of the drawing is comic, it features a racist depiction of a Native American as a disheveled, welfare-dependent drunk while positing the idea that genocide is something worthy of a good chuckle. *Library of Congress*

if candidate X is a hypocrite, this has no bearing on the validity/invalidity of either Libertarian economic principles or government agriculture subsidies. The validity/invalidity of both concepts exists outside of, and separate from, any one person's hypocrisies. Although pointing out someone's hypocrisy is used as a way to discredit their ideas or views, it is actually a criticism of the person's inconsistency and is a form of ad hominem attack (see chapter 4).

Deceptive Images

The old adage holds that "seeing is believing." Of course, anyone who is familiar with digital technology knows that you cannot believe everything you see. As pointed out in chapter 2, digital technology has made it easier than ever to manipulate photographs and video to mislead. But other types images can mislead as well.

Charts can easily mislead when they are based on bad data or are simply used in ways that are not well suited for their intended purpose. For example, even though pie charts frequently show up in popular media, they are avoided by statisticians because they are a poor choice for comparing sizes, especially when a pie chart contains a number of small slices (see figure 3.3).

Another type of image that can deceive is the map. Because maps are representations of reality, rather than reality itself, the ways in which they are drawn can mislead, either by intention or inadvertently. For example, consider the familiar Mercator projection map. Mercator projection maps are useful for navigation because they render latitude and longitude as a square grid, thereby allowing navigators to follow a straight compass heading from point A to point B without being thrown off course by the curvature of the earth. The problem with the Mercator projection, however, is that land masses closer to the equator appear smaller (and therefore less geopolitically significant) than they actually are (see figure 3.4).

A more recent example of potentially deceptive maps are the red state/blue state maps used to depict US election results. One problem with such maps is that showing an entire state as either 100 percent red or 100 percent blue ignores the fact that even the reddest of red states have significant numbers of blue voters and vice versa. For example, in the 2016 US presidential election, the solidly blue state of California voted for Democrat Hillary Clinton by a comfortable margin of 61.6 percent versus 32.8 percent for Republican Donald Trump. Even so, the fact remains that around 4.5 million Californians voted for Donald Trump. Meanwhile, in the solidly red state of Texas, 3.8 million Texans voted for Clinton. Coloring California all blue and Texas all red visually erases the votes of over eight million Americans. Another example of a deceptive election map occurs when votes are taken down to the county level with each county shown as either red or blue. Not only do such maps replicate the 100 percent fallacy of the red state/blue state maps, but such maps also fail to acknowledge the vastly different populations of US counties.

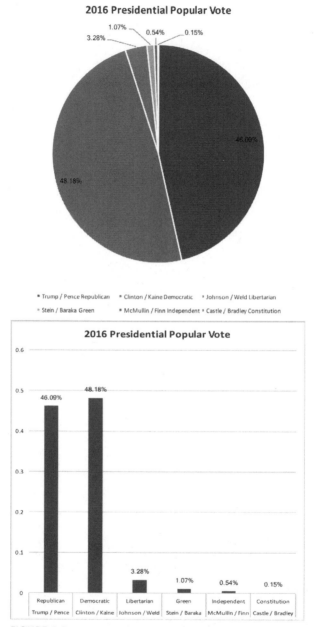

FIGURE 3.3
In the this example, visually comparing popular vote percentages among several candidates is much easier with the bar chart than with the pie chart. *Donald A. Barclay*

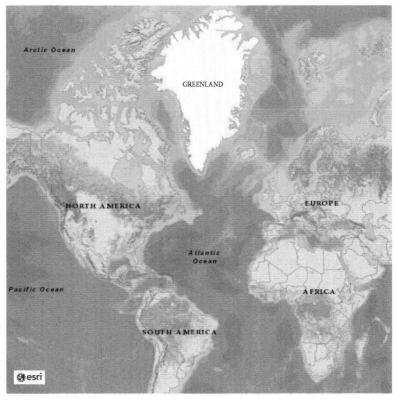

FIGURE 3.4
Because this map uses the Mercator projection, it is impossible to tell that Africa is, in fact, fourteen times the size of Greenland. *Donald A. Barclay*

Because the most populous US counties have millions of residents while the smallest number less than one hundred inhabitants, showing every county as equal creates a wildly distorted picture of how the nation actually voted.

Emphasizing Outliers

Emphasizing an outlier is a neat trick because it can be used with information that is actually credible. One way this trick works is by presenting an extreme case—an outlier—so as to discredit a large segment of the population. Example:

A college newspaper editor wrote an opinion piece that says college tuition should be free for everyone.

That editor is a Millennial.

Those spoiled Millennials think the world owes them a free college education.

Assume the first and second statements are true. Does that make the third statement true? Only if the opinion of the college newspaper editor is representative of all, or at least most, Millennials. The only way to determine that would be by conducting a scientifically valid opinion survey of Millennials. If the newspaper editor is an outlier whose opinion represents only a few Millennials, then the third statement is misleading.

Even though people should be able to see through the trick of propping up outliers as representative of larger groups, this technique is nonetheless widely used for smearing entire populations ranging from gun owners to college professors to suburban soccer moms. No conclusion about any group of people should be based on the views or actions of an outlier (or two or three), whose views and actions may be not at all representative of the larger group.

Beyond smearing groups, the outlier trick can be used to mislead people about an issue or a cause. People who oppose seat belt laws are quick to point to the very rare instances in which someone survived a car crash because they were not wearing a seat belt. While such cases occur from time to time, they are such outliers that focusing on them while ignoring the tens of thousands of verified cases in which seat belts save lives and prevent injuries is as dishonest as it is misleading.

Faking Expertise

This trick involves falsely claiming—or falsely crediting someone else with—expertise and then using that fake expertise to support an argument. How can you tell if someone is actually an expert on the topic in question?

It is a bad sign if an expert is not named and is instead described in a generic way, such as "a leading forensic examiner" or "an expert on international trade" or "an industry analyst." Even when a name is given, watch out when the alleged expert's qualifications are of the sort that anyone could claim with impunity. For example, just about anyone could claim to be "a commentator on the topic of natural foods and health," while not just anyone could rightfully claim to be "a registered dietician with a PhD in human nutrition from Johns Hopkins University." A superficially meaningful credential that frequently gets misused is "journalist." While the word *journalist* could be applied to someone with an MBA, two decades of actual business experience, and a paid position writing a weekly personal finance column for the *Wall Street Journal*, it could also describe someone whose entire journalistic experience consists of a personal blog and a few posts to unmoderated comments sections. There is no more a law against calling yourself a journalist than there is against calling yourself a poet or a mime.

INSTANT EXPERTISE: JUST MIX AND MATCH THESE PUFFED-UP ADJECTIVES WITH CORRESPONDING MEANINGLESS CREDENTIALS

Adjective	Credential
noted	blogger
recognized	expert
celebrated	authority
acknowledged	consultant
well-known	speaker
experienced	professional

As mentioned in chapter 2, expertise in one area does not automatically bestow expertise in another. When anyone is presented as, or claims to be, an expert, it is worth asking is whether they are an expert on the topic in question. Someone who has flown crop dusters for twenty years is not necessarily an expert on airline transportation. A distinguished scientist who studies antibiotic-resistant bacteria is not necessarily an expert on preschool education.

Experience and education are both factors in determining expertise, but phony experts can make false claims regarding either or both.

To check up on an expert's professional experience, visit the website of the university, agency, or business for which the expert claims to work to see if there is any mention of her name, position, responsibilities, or qualifications. You can also try entering the expert's name—along with her place of employment and/or line of work—into a web search engine to see if you can find independent (i.e., not created by the person you are checking out) verification of the individual's professional experience. If you have access (possibly through your public or school library) to periodical databases, then newspaper and magazine articles provide another way to check out someone's claims to expertise. In the twenty-first century, just about anyone prominent enough in any line of work to be considered an expert is likely to be mentioned (by impartial sources) in magazines, in newspapers, or on the web. If an expert claims to be an academic—a professor or an academic researcher—then a search of Google Scholar (scholar.google.com) should turn up at least a few scholarly articles or books written by that expert on the topic in question.

Here's an academic pro tip: not everyone who teaches at a college or university is a professor. The title of "professor" is generally reserved for full-time, permanent faculty members of a college or university. Non-professors who teach at a college or university have titles like "lecturer" or "adjunct" or "non-tenure-track faculty." Just because a college or university teacher is not a professor does not mean he cannot be an expert, but if someone who is not actually a professor claims that title, he or she is not being fully honest.

Educational qualifications can be tricky to check out. People can straight-up lie about their education and get away with it for years. If an expert claims to have a degree from a specific college or university, verifying the truth of that statement can be difficult. However, if someone claims to have a doctorate-level degree (PhD, DPhil., EdD., etc.), it almost certainly means the person wrote a dissertation, which is something you can check out fairly easily. First, search the expert's name (and the school that awarded the doctorate, if known) in the free OCLC WorldCat database (www.worldcat.org). WorldCat allows you to limit search results to only dissertations, greatly reducing the number of hits retrieved. If the dissertation does not turn up in WorldCat and you know the name of the college or university that awarded the degree, go to the online library catalog of that college or university and search for the dissertation there. If the dissertation does not turn up in either source, you may be looking at someone who is claiming a doctoral degree that was never earned.

Medical doctors (MD or DO) do not write dissertations unless they also hold a PhD, so searching for a dissertation is not helpful for determining if someone claiming to be a medical doctor actually is. However, you can turn to the American Medical Association's online Doctor Finder database (apps .ama-assn.org/doctorfinder/home.jsp), which contains information on "virtually every licensed physician in the United States." Other countries may or may not have similar online directories of physicians.

Another trick of the fake expert is to hold worthless diploma-mill degrees from unaccredited colleges or universities. The US Department of Education maintains a searchable database of accredited US colleges and universities (www.ed.gov/accreditation) that you can search to see if a US institution is accredited or not. If the institution from which the degree was earned is based outside of the United States, it is possible the country in question maintains online lists of accredited institutions located within its borders.

Finally, even when an expert is well qualified to comment on the topic in question, it is crucial to remember that experts do not always agree with each other. The word of a single expert, no matter how well qualified, is never the final word on any topic.

Falsifying Attribution

One sign of credible information is that it is accurately attributed to a real and credible source. When such attribution is lacking, the information may not be credible. The act of attributing a piece of information to a source (such as a book, a website, an article, a person, etc.) is called *citing* and the information that identifies the source is call a *citation*. Citations can be informal: "President Franklin D. Roosevelt said, 'We have nothing to fear but fear itself.'" Or citations can follow strict formatting guidelines like those found in the notes section at the end of this book.

Unattributed information lacks any citations identifying its sources. Things like eyewitness accounts and personal reflections may not require sources, but when someone presents information that goes beyond personal experience or common knowledge (see chapter 2), then sources are required if the information is credible.

It is always a red flag when information is attributed to ambiguous sources described with such inexact terms as *they, top scientists, an official, local police, many people, government documents, published reports, groundbreaking studies, archival footage,* and the like. Credible information cites named individuals or specific information sources:

Seattle Police Chief Kathleen O'Toole confirmed in a July 7, 2016, press conference . . .

On June 19, 2017, Goldman Sachs CEO Lloyd Blankfein reported in a televised interview that . . .

The 2016 United States Supreme Court case of *Welch v. United States* holds that . . .

As depicted in the 1965 documentary film *Tokyo Olympiad*, midcentury Japanese society was . . .

There are cases in which the use of anonymous sources can be legitimate, as when the identity of a whistleblower needs to be protected; even so, an anonymous source is still a red flag as far as the credibility of the information goes. At the very least, when an anonymous source is being used in a legitimate way, the creator of the information should acknowledge that the source is anonymous and provide a reasonable explanation as to why the source cannot be disclosed.

Another way to deceive is by falsely attributing information to a source that is, in fact, not the actual source of that information. One form this can take is that of attributing information to a completely made-up source. Users of this trick can give unsupported information the appearance of credibility by inventing individuals, organizations, or documents; citing them as sources; and hoping that nobody bothers to check up on their validity:

According to Mr. Ben Dover, director of the Federal Bureau of Keeping It Real, each year over 1,500 American public-school children between the ages of six and eleven fall victim to unprovoked noogie attacks.

Yet another form of false attribution is to credit as a source someone or something that has no connection to the information in question, as was the case when the author of the Moon Hoax articles of 1835 (discussed in chapter 2 of this book) claimed that the astronomer Sir John Herschel was the source of information for the articles.[5] The digital world has given rise to a rash of celebrity memes in which quotations, often inspirational, are attributed to famous people who never said any such thing. The actress Marilyn Monroe has become, for reasons unknown, a magnet for being credited with things she never said.[6]

While researching this book, I came across a perfect quotation about information that I was dying to use:

> True genius resides in the capacity for evaluation of uncertain, hazardous, and conflicting information.

This quotation appears on tens of thousands of websites, in newspaper and magazine articles, and even in scholarly books and journal articles. Every source that uses the quotation—and I checked out dozens and dozens of them—attributes the quotation to former British prime minister Winston Churchill; however, none of these users of the quotation provides a citation to its source. If the words are Churchill's, they have to be from something that can be cited: an identifiable speech, a conversation, or something Churchill put down in writing. If the words are Churchill's, there has to be a date associated with when he said or wrote them. A quotation cannot exist in a vacuum. I spent hours trying to determine if the quotation could truly be attributed to Churchill without finding any solid proof that he was the source. While proving a negative is difficult, unless new information to the contrary surfaces I have to believe that Churchill never said the words so widely and frequently attributed to him. This appears to be yet another case of a misattributed quotation that spreads from one source to another without anyone bothering to check the facts of the matter.

Alternatively, it is possible to cite a source in support of an argument when, in fact, the source does no such thing. For example, someone might cite Albert Einstein's seminal article, "On the Electrodynamics of Moving Bodies,"[7] which focuses on the concept of special relativity, to support their argument that the sun actually circles Earth. Of course, the problem with such a citation is that "On the Electrodynamics of Moving Bodies" in no way supports such an argument.

Finally, it is important to remember that citing one or more (even many more) noncredible sources of information does not somehow make the information that cites them credible. Sadly, the chore of thoroughly evaluating a piece of information may involve going down the rabbit hole of evaluating the sources it cites.

(Mis)Playing with Words

Suppose you received an unsolicited email with the following subject line:

An Important Message from Concerned Citizens for Freedom and Justice

Because phrases like *concerned citizens*, and words like *freedom* and *justice*, are so general that they can mean very different things to different people, it is impossible to tell from the name of this group if the position of its membership sits on the left, center, or right. Or, quite possibly, if their position is located more in the vicinity of Rigel 12. Using words that invoke positive or negative values while remaining on a high level of generality—words like *patriotism*, *liberty*, *terrorism*, *tyranny*, or *love*—is a way to slip a highly partisan message in front of those who might otherwise not give the message a second look if its bias was clear from the outset.

Another misuse of words is to throw around dismissive labels as a way of discrediting someone's point without having to go to the trouble of actually addressing that point. In contemporary political discourse, it is common to see labels such *fascist*, *libtard*, *Nazi*, *social justice warrior*, and much worse tossed around with abandon. Of course, such behavior is nothing new. A quick flip back through the pages of history reveals an almost endless list of dismissive labels, including racial and ethnic slurs, political insults, and nationalistic taunts. If someone makes a compelling argument or presents credible facts, dropping an insulting label on that person does not negate their argument or invalidate their facts.

There is also the linguistic trick of misleading through equivocation, hairsplitting, or resorting to legalisms, none of which are necessarily easy to spot without access to all the relevant information. Take the example of a public official vigorously denying accusations of accepting a $100,000 bribe (because the bribe was only $50,000). While the objection is technically correct, it is an equivocation because the point is not the size of the bribe; it is the fact that a bribe was accepted at all. It's a bit like a child telling his mother that he ate a serving of fruit when the serving of fruit was actually a bag of strawberry-flavored candy. Another example of this type of hairsplitting would be the backers of a ballot initiative promising that its passage will not impact the state's budget while failing to mention that this will only result if their wildly optimistic revenue projections hold true for the next thirty years. For those who employ equivocation, hairsplitting, and legalisms, there is always the slightest shred of truth to their words, but for all practical purposes their words are lies.

Misusing History

It is quite common to point to events or people from history to validate arguments about modern-day issues. As with any persuasive technique, appealing to history can be used to mislead.

The most basic abuse of history is simply getting the facts wrong, either through ignorance or intentionally. For example, someone might argue,

> Women did not fly military aircraft in World War II. Therefore, they should not be allowed to fly military aircraft today.

Besides tacitly implying that people in the past were somehow inherently wiser and better than people living today, the statement is historically inaccurate. Russian women flew combat missions during the war, while in the United States the more than one thousand WASPs (Women Airforce Service Pilots) ferried military aircraft all across the country. Whenever information presents something as a historical fact, it is worth making sure that the alleged fact is accurate.

A second abuse of history occurs when someone cherry-picks a historical fact or quotation—often taking it out of context—to support an argument. Take for example the following fact and conclusion:

> Mark Twain (Samuel L. Clemens) served in the Confederate military during the Civil War.

> This proves that Twain was a racist who supported slavery.

While the question of the extent to which Mark Twain did or did not hold racist views is a valid topic of scholarly debate, the preceding conclusion takes its supporting fact completely out of context:

- Twain served in a ragtag volunteer Confederate unit for less than two weeks before he headed off to Nevada.
- As far as is known, Twain never fired a shot in anger.
- Twain spent most of his long life writing works critical of slavery, racism, American imperialism, and the slave-owning culture that he saw as the root cause of the Civil War.

In context, Twain's brief military service is an anomaly that stands in contrast to every belief he espoused through his writing and the way he lived his life. Focusing on a few historical facts—or a few selected words of a historical figure—without considering the broader historical context is a dishonest use of history. If you selectively consider the historical examples of RMS *Titanic* and RMS *Lusitania*, you might conclude that crossing the Atlantic by steamship was an extremely perilous undertaking in the early decades of the twentieth century. However, if you consider all the thousands of ships that steamed back and forth across the Atlantic with no loss of life, your conclusion would be that crossing the Atlantic by steamship involved minimal risk.

Mixing Fact and Fiction

Misinformation often mixes in some amount of fact with greater or lesser amounts of fiction. This is especially true of propaganda, but less extreme forms of misinformation employ this trick as well. Suppose that a blog post contains the following statements:

Stanley Kubrick was a twentieth-century film director whose work won three BAFTA awards, one Academy Award, and one Golden Globe.

Kubrick's *2001: A Space Odyssey* included scenes of space travel that were far more realistic than anything audiences had seen prior to that time.

Danny Torrance, the child character in Kubrick's *The Shining*, wears a sweater depicting a rocket ship and displaying the words *Apollo 11* and *USA*.

Stanley Kubrick filmed the faked Apollo moon landings.

The first three statements are verifiably credible; the fourth is not. Presenting one or more highly credible facts can be an effective technique for getting people to accept any noncredible information along for the ride.

Omitting Selected Facts

Did you see the *New York Times* story about two hundred people in the town of Patchogue, New York, celebrating the birthday of Adolf Hitler? Terrible, right? Society is clearly falling apart when Nazis can run wild in a town not even sixty miles from the heart of Manhattan.

Hang on. The story is missing a few key facts:

- The celebration took place on April 20, 1944.
- The theme of the celebration was "Hitler's Last Birthday," and the refreshments served included deviled eggs, deviled ham, and devil's food cake.
- The party was put on by the local USO for the entertainment of US servicemen, with dance music provided by a band from a nearby US Army camp.[8]

This example shows how telling only part of a story can completely alter its meaning. Leaving out key facts about when, where, or why something happened is an all-too-common tool of deception. (By the way, the celebration was premature. Hitler lived just long enough to see one additional birthday.)

Documentary films stand out as a type of information often criticized for telling only part of a story (i.e., telling only the part the filmmakers want their audience to know). For example, the 2015 Netflix documentary *Making a Murderer*, which convinced thousands of viewers that an innocent man had been framed for murder, remains controversial because of claims by the local prosecutor and county sheriff (among others) that the documentary omitted details justifying the guilty verdict handed down by the jury.[9] While leaving out critical information can be a valid criticism of documentary films (as well as other types of information), it is also true that including every fact and point of view is at least difficult, if not impossible, especially in a medium like film in which there is a limited amount of time to tell a story and a limited production budget with which to tell it. The really important question when evaluating information is to ask whether the creator of the information has omitted credible facts and evidence that, if included, could substantially change how the recipients of the information understand and respond to it.

Pitting Us against Them

Whether the information is about *us* and *our* greatness or *them* and *their* evil ways, presenting information in ways that play into group loyalties and exaggerate group difference is an excellent means of catching people with their information guards down. The *us-versus-them* strategy is often on display in schoolyard and workplace rumors, in propaganda, and in the social-media echo chamber phenomenon that is part of the larger fake news phenomenon.

Privileging Eyewitness Accounts

Eyewitness accounts are often presented as slam-dunk proofs of credibility. Who can argue with, "I was there. I saw it with my own eyes."? Actually, there are excellent arguments against assuming eyewitness accounts are inevitably accurate, and a growing body of social science research casts serious doubt on the reliability of eyewitness testimony.[10] Human beings are not perfect, unbiased recording machines, so what they report having seen is shaped by their biases, preconceived ideas, and the influence of others, including fellow witnesses and investigators. There is no better evidence of the imperfection of eyewitness testimony than the fact that the accounts presented by legitimate eyewitnesses to the same event can differ from, or even contradict, each other. For an example of this, look no further than a baseball coach arguing with an umpire over a play that just unfolded right in front of their wide-open eyes.

Besides being mistaken about, or differently interpreting, what they saw, eyewitnesses can straight-up lie. Witnesses can be bribed or intimidated or feel that lying is justified "in this case." There are also many examples of people providing "eyewitness" accounts—often in writing—of events they never actually witnessed. For example, the aftermath of the 9/11 terror attacks saw cases of individuals providing detailed eyewitness accounts of the attacks when they were, in fact, nowhere near either the World Trade Center or the Pentagon.[11]

Of course, eyewitness accounts are not always wrong and constitute an important source of evidence for both historical and current events. However, such accounts need to be considered in light of all the facts and evidence and not given top priority just because someone claims to have been there and seen the whole thing. If one person claims, "I was outside the World Trade Center on 9/11, and I didn't see any planes hit the buildings," this claim has to be taken in context with the thousands who did report seeing airplanes, the video footage of airplanes hitting the buildings, and other corroborating evidence.

GROWING UP WITH AN EYEWITNESS TO HISTORY

During World War II, my father served as a sergeant in the US Army Infantry and was involved in ground combat in the Pacific Theater. He talked openly about his wartime experiences and shared many of his eyewitness accounts of the war with me. Do I believe every war story my father told me? To quote Mark Twain's *Adventures of Huckleberry Finn*, "There was things which he stretched, but mainly he told the truth."

So, yes, I believe my father was a mostly reliable eyewitness, though I cannot swear that every word he said was the unvarnished truth. For example, a few years before he died my father told me a story about a wartime incident so extraordinary that I had a hard time believing him. For one thing, it was an entirely new war story that he had never before told, something quite unusual for him at that point in his life. The second thing was that the incident my father described seemed more like some incredible exploit pulled from a Captain America comic book than a true story. Of course, I did not tell my father that I doubted his story, but, in fact, I did.

Fast-forward a year. I was flipping through a library copy of historian Samuel Eliot Morison's *History of United States Naval Operations in World War II* when I came upon a description of an incident—an attempt by Japanese airborne troops to launch a surprise attack behind the American lines—that completely matched my father's hard-to-believe story. The location, the date, and the details as related by Morison comprised strong evidence that the incident my father described actually took place. Of course, the history book could not tell me if my father played the part he claimed to have played in this remarkable incident. Maybe he did. Or maybe he inserted himself into someone else's true story. Though my father's actual role in the incident is something that most likely can never be verified, I am inclined to believe his story is true while accepting that some part of it might be an invention.

The point of *my* story is that other people in our lives—family, friends, work colleagues, and schoolmates—regularly share information in the form of eyewitness accounts of events. Some of these events are trivial, "You should have seen the line at the grocery store this afternoon." Others are more dramatic, "Some maniac ran a stop sign and nearly T-boned me on the way to work." The natural human tendency is to accept as credible the eyewitness accounts of people you know. And, in most cases, that is the right thing to do. However, it is important to remember that the eyewitness accounts of people you respect, trust, like, and quite possibly love can be shaped by their biases, lapses of memory, and misinterpretations of what they have (or merely claim to have) seen. In the final analysis, the eyewitness account of someone you know is no more or no less credible than the eyewitness account of a complete stranger.

When I say that I do not believe *everything* my father told me about the things he witnessed in the war, I mean no disrespect to him. I am simply recognizing that he was a human being and not a perfectly impartial and infallible history-recording machine. Holding anyone to so high a standard of credibility is unreasonable and unfair. I also recognize that my own eyewitness accounts are as fallible as anyone else's and do my best to keep this in mind, especially when sharing my stories with those who I know are inclined to trust me.

Rankings and Reviews

Ranking and reviews can be useful sources of information, but they can also be used to mislead.

Rankings are most credible when they are based on clearly defined objective criteria. Ranking countries from smallest to largest based on their size in square kilometers constitutes credible ranking because the physical size of countries is not subject to much, if any, interpretation. On the other hand, ranking countries from worst to best based on their quality of life is quite subjective, though less so when the criteria used to calculate quality of life (income, cost of living, health, safety, political freedoms, etc.) are explicitly stated. One type of ranking that draws a great deal of attention is the ranking of colleges and universities, with students and their parents often making important, life-changing decisions based on such rankings. However, among those who study higher education, there is considerable dismay over the power of college and university rankings, in part because the data and methodologies used for the some of the rankings is not very good, in part because quantifying something as nuanced as what college or university is the best choice for any given student is a disservice to both students and colleges and universities.[12]

Reviews—whether of restaurants, films, hotels, or college professors—can be helpful for decision making, though it is important to recognize how subjective reviews can be. Almost everyone has experience the dismay of reading a review that is the dead opposite of their own experience: "Did the idiot who wrote this review even see the same movie I saw?" One question to ask of any review is, "What does this reviewer know about the thing being reviewed?" Even if I do not agree with its assessment, a review of a new automobile written by an automotive professional who has been behind the wheel of hundreds of different vehicles carries more weight than a review by someone whose knowledge of automobiles comes mostly from playing video games and watching action films. Another question to ask of any review is, "Is this reviewer too biased to be credible?" For example, it is possible for the owners of a local restaurant to use fake names to post either overly negative reviews of a competitor's restaurant or overly positive reviews of their own establishment. When evaluating reviews found in online sites to which anyone can contribute, it is generally a good idea to consider all the reviews as a whole rather than focusing on a few extremely positive or extremely negative reviews.

Repeating until It Is the Truth

For several decades now, social scientists have acknowledged the validity of a phenomenon known as the *truth effect*. In essence, the truth effect holds that the more something is repeated, the more likely people are to believe that it is true.[13] Because of the ease with which digital information can be copied and distributed, the online environment makes it easier than ever before for a piece of information to gain credibility through repetition. Many conspiracy theories, for example, gain credibility through sheer repetition.

As information is repeated, it is possible for a kind of circular attribution to take place. Pat cites Chris as a source of information. Chris cites Jesse. Jesse cites Pat and Chris. And on and on. Given time, circular attribution can give the appearance that information that started out with no credible source is supported by multiple sources and has become, somehow, credible.

Sharing Secrets

Almost everyone enjoys being in on a secret, enjoys the thrill of knowing some fact to which others are not privy. The pleasure of knowing, and revealing, secrets is why rumors, including false rumors, spread so quickly. The appeal of conspiracy theories, too, is partly about being in on a secret, of having access to the "straight dope" to which others are oblivious.

Want in on a secret *they* don't want *us* to know?

Here is some information to which all those dumb sheep out there are oblivious. Just us sly foxes are in on this.

Not everyone can handle the real truth, but we can.

Because being in on a secret that turns out to be untrue is not as much fun as being in on a secret that is true, people are inclined to believe secrets rather than to question their credibility. As for secrets shared in the online environment, how secret can they be when they are posted and reposted where (potentially) millions of people can access them?

Torturing Analogies

Analogies work by listing several properties shared by thing A and thing B, pointing out an additional property of thing B, and then arguing that thing A does—or could—have this further property. For example:

Shared properties:

- London and Manhattan are subject to unacceptably heavy traffic congestion.
- London and Manhattan do not have space to build additional roads.
- London and Manhattan offer extensive public-transportation options that people could use instead of driving their cars.

Further property:

- London has successfully reduced traffic by charging congestion pricing.

Conclusion:

- Manhattan could reduce traffic by charging congestion pricing.

    Now whether or not this conclusion is valid depends on several factors.

- The degree of relevant similarity between the things being compared:
    - In the example, the more London and Manhattan are similar in ways that are relevant to the conclusion, the more likely the analogy holds. This is why an analogy comparing London, United Kingdom, to Manhattan, New York, is more likely to hold than one comparing London, United Kingdom, to Manhattan, Kansas.
- The number of shared properties between the things compared as well as the variety of those properties:
    - The more properties London and Manhattan share, the more likely it is the analogy will hold. However, the number of properties are less significant if all the properties are similar. For example, if all the shared properties concerned only the capacity of the roads in each location while ignoring factors like public-transportation options, lifestyles, cultural

norms, and impact on surrounding communities, the less likely it is that the analogy will hold.
- The relevance of the shared properties to the conclusion:
  - If the similarities between London and Manhattan focus on things that are not relevant to traffic and transportation, the analogy is less likely to hold. The fact that world-class theater, restaurants, and art galleries are properties of both London and Manhattan is not all that relevant to each location's traffic problems.

Analogies, when used properly, can be powerful tools of persuasion. However, they can be misused to draw invalid conclusions. Keeping in mind how valid analogies work—and why invalid analogies fail—is the best defense against falling for tortured analogies that (1) compare things that are not really all that similar; (2) rely on lists of irrelevant, superficial shared properties; and (3) reach strained conclusions that do not hold up to careful examination.

Trolling

A creature of the Digital Age, the Internet troll is a person who stirs up trouble online by being aggressively argumentative and inflammatory for the purpose of upsetting others. Trolls may actually care about whatever arguments they put forward, or they may engage in trolling just for the fun they get from working strangers into a frenzy. Trolling happens in comment sections, on social media sites, and in just about any other public online forum. Not surprisingly, trolls do not have any qualms about simply making up information, so nothing trolls say should be accepted as credible information without first evaluating it. The anonymity of the digital world encourages trolling, as it is very unlikely that a troll will ever have to confront in the physical world someone they have tormented in the online world.

An early, and notorious, example of trolling unfolded in 1993 when the Usenet group alt.tasteless pranked the group rec.pet.cats by posting pseudo-innocent, yet tasteless, questions about caring for cats; eventually, the members of alt.tasteless escalated to such trollish outrages as exchanging recipes in which cat is the main ingredient.[14] Although the concept of trolling (in the online sense) was not widely known in 1993, the behavior of the members of alt.tasteless in front of the truly horrified, cat-loving members of rec.pet.cats stands as an early example of what would become the all-too-familiar practice of trolling.

THE DUNNING-KRUGER EFFECT

In the opening paragraphs of their seminal article "Unskilled and Unaware of It: How Difficulties in Recognizing One's Own Incompetence Lead to Self-Inflated Assessments," Cornell University psychologists Justin Kruger and David Dunning spell out what they acknowledge to be a harsh conclusion:

> We argue that when people are incompetent in the strategies they adopt to achieve success and satisfaction, they suffer a dual burden: Not only do they reach erroneous conclusions and make unfortunate choices, but their incompetence robs them of the ability to realize it. Instead . . . they are left with the mistaken impression that they are doing just fine.[15]

Does this phenomenon extend to evaluating information? The evidence suggests it does. One review article analyzing "53 English language studies that assessed and compared peoples' self-reported and demonstrated information literacy (IL) skills" found that the Dunning-Kruger effect applies to information literacy.[16] In other words, the research shows that many people are not as good at finding and evaluating information as they think they are, and their exaggerated self-confidence blinds them to their shortcomings.

The conclusion reached by this research confirms my own, non-scientific observations that students and others who are novices at working with information tend to view finding credible information as nothing more than typing a few words into Google and, all too often, do not think much about evaluating the information they find (assuming they evaluate that information at all). Maybe you are not one of those overly confident types and have a good understanding of your actual abilities. But then again, according to the findings of Dunning and Kruger it is unlikely that you would recognize that you are overly confident of your abilities. For anyone, it does not hurt to ask yourself if you "reach erroneous conclusions and make unfortunate choices" when it comes to evaluating and using information. Further, assuming you are able to recognize that you are not "doing just fine," are you willing to make the effort required to become more a competent evaluator and user of information?

RECAP

Creators of information have many deceptive tricks they can employ in the hope that you drop your information guard and fall for information that is not credible. Being aware of, and alert for, these tricks will help you avoid falling for them. That said, anyone can fall for misinformation, especially when encountering information that confirms existing biases or plays on emotions. Powerful emotions like anger, fear, and joy can be manipulated in ways that cause you to drop your information guard, so it is important to remain vigilant when you feel information evoking strong emotions. Similarly, being aware of your own limitations as an evaluator of information—and working to overcome those limitations—is key to avoid being tricked into accepting misleading information.

4

Logical Fallacies

More Tools of Deception

Logical fallacies are rhetorical devices misused for the purpose of persuasion. Some of the tricks described in the previous chapter could, and maybe should, be classified as logical fallacies. For example, the trick labeled "Denouncing Hypocrisy" is a form of the ad hominem logical fallacy described in this chapter. Even though there is some overlap among logical fallacies and the tricks described in chapter 3, the importance of learning to spot deceptive practices in their various guises justifies a bit of repetition.

However you classify them, logical fallacies are problematic in that they are built on errant reasoning that undermines the argument being made. Though logical fallacies cannot undermine an argument when you are aware that they are being used, they work all too well when they fly under your radar undetected. This is why learning to spot logical fallacies and understand their weaknesses is an important skill for evaluating information.

Logical fallacies have been used, and denounced, for centuries, as reflected by the fact that some are still best known by their Latin names. As old as they may be, logical fallacies continue to appear in both the print and the digital world. There are dozens of logical fallacies, but the focus here will be on those that surface most frequently. For anyone who is interested in learning more about logical fallacies, there are a number of sources that cover them in depth. The free *Stanford Encyclopedia of Philosophy* has a substantial scholarly article on fallacies (plato.stanford.edu/entries/fallacies). The Purdue OWL (Online

Writing Lab) is one of many university-affiliated websites offering lists of logical fallacies along with definitions and examples (owl.english.purdue.edu/owl/resource/659/03).

AD HOMINEM

A very common logical fallacy, the ad hominem attack focuses on some flaw in an individual rather than on that person's opinions or arguments. Example:

> Our principal is a bald old man who drives a boring car. Why should he be allowed to ban soda from the school?

Regardless of whether the principal should or should not ban soda from the school, attacks on his hair, age, and choice of transportation have no relevance to the wisdom of banning soda or whether the principal is qualified to make such a decision.

Figure 4.1 shows an ad hominem attack on President George W. Bush.

AD POPULUM

The *ad populum* fallacy appeals either to positive ideals (such as patriotism, liberty, or religion) or to their counterpoint negative fears (such as xenophobia, tyranny, sinfulness) in order to distract from the question actually being discussed. Example:

> If the school bans soda, the terrorists of ISIS win.

Of course, ISIS has no direct connection to soda being banned from schools (at least in schools outside of any territory ISIS controls), so bringing up ISIS in this context is simply a misdirection that plays on fear and patriotism.

APPEAL TO AUTHORITY

Also known by the Latin name *ad verecundiam*, this fallacy is based on deferring to a leader or an expert (qualified or not) because of who that person is or the position they hold. Example:

> If the chair of the National Soft Drink Council says that soda does not impact the health of schoolkids, then we should listen. Honestly, who knows more about soda?

FIGURE 4.1

This photo shows an example of ad hominem attack in which President George W. Bush is depicted as a prison inmate. In addition, his facial features (especially his ears) have been exaggerated to make him look unintelligent. Attacking the person, rather than what the person stands for, has been a staple of politics for centuries. *istock/ ScottKrycia*

The problem with appealing to authority is that simply being an authority does not make anyone the final word on any topic. Often, deferring to the opinion of one expert means ignoring the opinion of some other equally qualified expert.

BANDWAGON FALLACY

This fallacy argues that because an idea is popular, it is the right thing to do.

A survey of the student body shows that over 60 percent want to have soda on campus. The will of the people must be obeyed.

One need look no further than examples of mob rule to realize the majority is not always right. In many democratic countries, including the United

States, constitutions limit the power of the majority so that basic human rights are not subject to the tyranny of the majority.

CONFIRMATION BIAS

Confirmation bias describes the (very human) tendency to focus only on information that supports what you already believe while ignoring information that contradicts your beliefs. Example:

> My research on the subject turned up twenty-five articles proving that school soda bans do nothing to improve the health of students.

Yes, but what about all the articles showing that school soda bans have a positive impact on student health? Also, it is not the number of sources supporting or discrediting an argument that matters. It is the credibility of the information contained in those sources. A thousand online rants claiming that a popular recreational drug is harmless do not invalidate three rigorous scientific studies finding that the drug can have serious adverse effects.

DISMISSIVE FALLACY

This fallacy operates on the idea of dismissing something simply because it seems absurd or does not conform to some ill-defined concept of common sense. Example:

> Banning soda from the school is just weird and ridiculous.

Common sense is a highly subjective concept, so the fact that something strikes an individual, or even a group of individuals, as weird, absurd, or unusual does not make it false. Not owning a car may seem absurd to someone who lives in a small town or a midsized city, but it may not seem at all odd to someone who lives in a crowded urban center such as Tokyo or Paris.

DIVINE FALLACY

This fallacy involves attributing anything that cannot be readily explained to some supernatural power. Example:

> The reason for the soda ban is that an evil spirit has taken control of the principal's soul. There is no other explanation.

While supernatural intervention is not *necessarily* ruled out as the cause, neither is it proven by the claim there is no other explanation. Even though they may not be known, there could be many other explanations for the principal's behavior. A similar example occurs when strange, unexplainable lights appear in the sky and people automatically assume the source must be alien spacecraft. Alien spacecraft *may* be the source of the lights, but this is not proven by the lack of some other explanation.

EITHER/OR

Reducing options to an either/or choice oversimplifies complicated questions for which there may be multiple solutions. Example:

> Either we stop this soda ban or we will all die of thirst.

Or the students could drink water at school. Or drink enough liquid at breakfast to get through the end of the school day without perishing. Reducing a problem to two stark choices may be an effective way to rabble-rouse, but most problems do not boil down to simple either/or choices. Couching choices in such reductionist terms only serves to inhibit creative problem solving.

Figure 4.2 shows an either/or scenario that ultimately proved false.

GENETIC FALLACY

This fallacy condemns by implying that the origin of a person, idea, theory, and so on determines its worth or credibility. Example:

> There's a weird religious cult in Southern California that doesn't allow its members to drink soda. The plan to ban soda is cult based and must be stopped.

Whether or not a cult allows soda has no bearing on health-related arguments put forward as the reason for removing soda from the school. The genetic fallacy is often invoked to criticize such phenomena as antismoking campaigns and vegetarianism on the grounds that both were embraced by some leaders of Nazi Germany. Or course neither antismoking campaigns nor vegetarianism have any direct connection to the horrors perpetrated during the Third Reich. One could as easily argue that, because the first modern

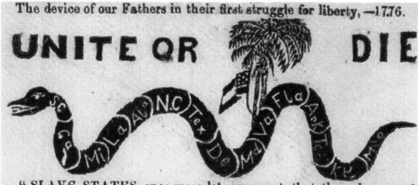

FIGURE 4.2
This image from the US Civil War proposes an either/or scenario that proved false. In fact, several of the states depicted on the snake—Missouri, Delaware, Maryland, and Kentucky—never joined the Confederacy and, of course, still exist to this day. *Library of Congress*

freeway system, the autobahn, was built under Nazi rule, freeways are therefore morally objectionable and should be banned.

HASTY GENERALIZATION
This occurs when someone jumps to a conclusion based on biased or insufficient evidence. Example:

> The soda ban has been in place for a month, but the students are as unhealthy as ever. It's not working.

Maybe the soda ban will result in healthier students. Maybe not. A month is not enough time to know. Similar examples include such hasty generalizations as jumping to conclusions about a sports team's championship potential based on the outcome of the first game of the season or predicting the long-term success of a new restaurant based on its first few weeks in business.

MORAL EQUIVALENCE

One of the Internet's oldest "laws" is Godwin's law, which can be paraphrased as "Any online argument that goes on long enough will eventually invoke Hitler." The point of Godwin's law is similar to the point of the moral equivalence fallacy: it is logically flawed to trivialize something terrible, such as the Holocaust, by comparing it to something much less serious. Example:

> Banning soda from the school is the greatest injustice since the Tiananmen Square massacre!

No, it is not. Not even close. Making a faulty analogy—equating things that are not really comparable—regularly rears its head in heated debates. Athletes not being paid for participating in college sports may or may not be unfair, but it is not the equivalent of slavery. Living in a cramped studio apartment is not ideal, but it is not the equivalent of being locked up in solitary confinement.

PACKAGE DEAL FALLACY

Commonly used in political arguments, this fallacy assumes that beliefs that traditionally go together always go together. Example:

> Jane is a vegan and runs on the track team. You better believe she is all for the soda ban.

Not necessarily. Jane might believe that the soda ban is an affront to individual liberty and disagree with it in spite of her personal dietary and health choices. Similarly, someone who would not dream of owning a gun might support the Second Amendment. Or a married couple who have chosen not to have children of their own might support both extended parental leave and free child care for working parents. There is nothing that prevents a person from holding views that others see as contradictory, though anyone who does so runs the risk of being attacked as a hypocrite.

POST HOC

Formally known as *post hoc ergo propter hoc*, this logical fallacy underpins the "Confounding Correlation with Causation" trick described in chapter 3.

The (faulty) reasoning of this fallacy is simple: thing A came before thing B. Therefore, thing A caused thing B. Example:

> First they put a salad bar in the school lunchroom. A month later they decided to ban soda. The salad bar is the reason they banned soda.

While installing a salad bar and banning soda may both have been motivated by concerns about student health and nutrition, without evidence of causation there is no reason to conclude that the earlier occurrence caused the latter.

RED HERRING
The red herring is a misdirection technique that distracts from the relevant issue. Example:

> If you think the soda ban is a good thing, then how do you explain the increase in students getting detentions?

The relevant issue here is the soda ban, not student behavior. Without an established connection between the two, the rate of student detentions is not relevant. A version of the red herring fallacy is the "what about" tactic, in which someone tries to change the topic by bringing up some unrelated topic:

> Your honor, we have obtained video evidence of you accepting a bribe from an attorney who is currently pleading a case in your court.

> Yeah, but what about all those so-called homeless people aggressively panhandling on our streets and sleeping in doorways?

SLIPPERY SLOPE
The slippery slope fallacy argues that if you allow W to happen, then X, Y, and Z are the inevitable consequences. Example:

> If this soda ban is put in place, the next thing you know they will ban chips, gum, and cell phones. And from there it is only a short step to mandatory school uniforms.

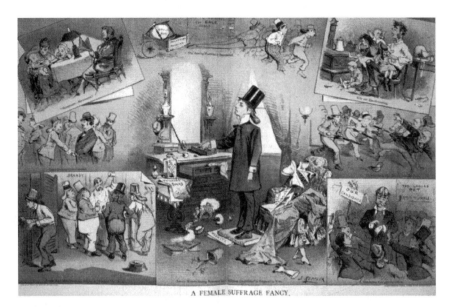

FIGURE 4.3
This anti–women's suffrage cartoon paints a slippery slope scenario in which women winning the right to vote has inevitably led to a complete reversal of male and female roles. *Library of Congress*

While such an outcome is (remotely) possible, it is far from inevitable. The slippery slope fallacy is a type of a non sequitur (Latin for "it does not follow"). A non sequitur occurs when a conclusion does not necessary follow from what precedes it: "Since the state legislature passed that bill decriminalizing marijuana, there is no doubt they will raise college tuition" (see figure 4.3 for another example).

STRAW MAN

This logical fallacy takes several forms, the most common of which involves attacking an argument that an opponent never raised.

> The principal's soda ban will not reduce littering on campus because 100 percent of soda cans on campus are recycled.

This is a straw man attack because the principal has never argued that the soda ban was about reducing littering; instead, his point is that a soda ban will improve the health of students.

RECAP

Logical fallacies often appear in information focusing on political and social controversies. While the existence of a logical fallacy does not necessarily mean that the information in which it is used is completely noncredible, logical fallacies undermine the specific arguments they are employed to support. Being familiar with logical fallacies and alert to their use will help you become a better evaluator of information and help you keep up your information guard in the face of deceptive arguments.

Evaluating an Information Source

Nine Essential Questions Everyone Should Ask

The most basic question for anyone trying to evaluate information is "How credible is this information?" While there is no simple formula for evaluating any given piece of information, the following list of questions constitutes a reasonable line of inquiry for establishing the credibility of any information you may encounter.

When evaluating information, it is important to remember that most information falls on a continuum somewhere between completely noncredible and incontrovertible fact, with relatively little information resting at one extreme or the other. It is similarly important to remember that when you are evaluating a piece of information no single factor is necessarily a deal maker or a deal breaker. Evaluation is more about looking at the whole package and making an informed judgment about the information's credibility than it is about rooting out a single factor that makes the case one way or the other. For example, suppose a documentary filmmaker who has never before done any work on the topic of terrorism suddenly releases a one-hour documentary on that topic. Does that one fact—the filmmaker's lack of experience with the topic of terrorism—discredit the film? Not necessarily. While it would be worth asking, "Is someone who has never before addressed the topic of terrorism qualified to make such a film?" other factors may add to the film's credibility: Maybe the filmmaker took an entire year to study terrorism and consulted with a number of terrorism experts as preparation for shooting the film. Maybe the filmmaker has produced several documentaries about violence and violent behavior and therefore shooting a film about terrorism is not that much of a stretch. Maybe the film has been well reviewed with many and varied reviewers commenting on the film's credibility.

Reiterating the point: evaluating any given piece of information is about looking at the whole picture rather than focusing on a single factor that, somehow, proves or disproves credibility.

QUESTION 1: WHO CREATED THE INFORMATION?

When evaluating any piece of information, arguably the most important question you can ask is "What can I learn about the knowledge, experience, reputation, and outlook of the person or persons who wrote, drew, filmed, or otherwise created this information?" There are a number of steps you can take to answer questions about the author, or authors, of information. (For the sake of brevity, I will use the word *author* broadly to include any creator of information in any format, including videos, images, data sets, etc.)

Is the author anonymous or is the authorship wrongly attributed to someone who did not actually create the information?

- If the answer to either question is yes, then the credibility of the information itself must be seriously questioned.
- There are cases where anonymous authorship is legitimate, as when the creators of the information might be harmed or possibly killed if their identities were revealed, but even in such cases anonymous information should be approached with a high degree of skepticism.

Is there objective biographical information addressing the author's qualifications?

- Have articles about the author been published in newspapers, magazines, reference works, news websites, or other sources that are not under the author's control?

Is the author knowledgeable about the topic in question?

- Is the author a genuine expert on the topic? (See "Faking Expertise" in chapter 3 for suggestions on how to determine whether or not someone is a qualified expert.)

- Has the author produced other credible works (books, articles, videos, etc.) on or related to the topic in question? Note: Having produced a large number of poorly researched, heavily biased, and generally noncredible works on a topic does not make someone an expert on that topic.

Is there a possible conflict of interest?

- Does the author have a financial, personal, or political interest that could cause the author to be less than completely forthcoming?
- Another way of framing the conflict-of-interest question is to simply ask, "Who benefits?" (You can even impress your friends by using the Latin version of this question: *Cui bono?*)

For example, if the CEO of a company writes an article encouraging people to buy shares in her company, she clearly has a financial interest in presenting her company in the best possible light and will benefit if people read her article and invest in her company. While this does not necessarily mean the information is not credible—the CEO may run a great company that represents a sound investment opportunity—it does mean you have to question the author's impartiality. The same caution would apply if, for example, you have a university president praising the quality of education at his campus during a television interview or a US senator publicly promoting support for a bill that she authored.

QUESTION 2: WHO PUBLISHED THE INFORMATION?

As with the word *author*, I will use the word *publisher* very broadly to include any entity—whether private, governmental, or nonprofit—that serves to put information in front of the public. (At the risk of pointing out the obvious, the words *publisher* and *public* come from the same Latin root.) Publishers' outlets include newspapers, magazines, journals, books, films, broadcast media, websites, and social-media platforms.

Does the publisher have a known bias?

- For example, the political magazine the *Nation* has a liberal bias while its rival publication, the *National Review*, has a conservative bias. Being published by a source with a bias does not invalidate information. However, the existence of a bias means that opposing points of view will likely be downplayed or completely missing. In the most extreme cases, the publisher's bias can be so strong that the information sinks to the level of propaganda.

Does the publisher have a reputation for credibility?

- Publishers who set high standards for editorial processes and fact-checking develop reputations for credibility. Those who cut corners or simply do not care about credibility, do not.
- Getting a sense of any publisher's reputation is not always easy. It cannot be based on any one person's opinion. On one hand, anyone who has ever disagreed with or felt wronged by a publisher will very likely label the publisher as biased, unfair, or inaccurate—even in cases where the publisher was providing credible information. On the other hand, anyone who is in sympathy with the publisher's aims will likely label the publisher a credible source. It typically requires looking at the opinions of a number of diverse commentators in order to get a sense of a publisher's overall reputation.
- Even a good reputation for credibility does not ensure that every piece of information appearing under a credible publisher's banner is automatically trustworthy. Two examples of discredited information mentioned in chapter 2—Walter Duranty's reports on the famine in the Soviet Union and the "Jimmy's World" hoax—were published in, respectively, the highly regarded *New York Times* and the equally esteemed *Washington Post*. Even though both of these publications have excellent reputations for accurate reporting and fact-checking, their good reputations do not render either one infallible.
- Publishers' reputations can change over time. Factors such as changes in ownership, declining revenues, competition from new media outlets (such as social media), and political pressure can impact a publisher's ability and/ or willingness to maintain the highest standards of credibility.

Does the publisher have experience with the topic in question?

- Publishers who focus on a particular topic are probably (though not necessarily always) better sources of information on that topic than publishers who only dabble in it. For example, the health information website MedlinePlus (medlineplus.gov) has years of experience providing health information to the public and is, therefore, more likely to be a reliable source of health information than, say, a website devoted to rebuilding classic cars.

Does the publisher have a conflict of interest?

- As with authors, publishers can be influenced by conflicts of interest. For example, information published on the website of a trade association representing motorcycle manufacturers is very likely to promote motorcycling as a safe and enjoyable form of transportation while downplaying the risks.
- One of the most obvious and prevalent conflicts of interest is between publishers and advertisers, as publishers are loath to publish anything that might cause advertisers to pull their financial support. Indeed, some argue that accepting any advertising revenue at all fatally compromises a publisher's ability to produce unbiased, fully credible information.
- Government websites, which typically do not carry advertising, have built-in conflicts of interest as well. The NASA website is likely to promote the interests of NASA while being unlikely to provide information advocating that the NASA budget should be cut. Similarly, a state legislator's official web page is unlikely to provide information supporting bills he or she opposes.

Information provided by any publisher or author who operates under one or more conflicts of interest is not automatically invalid. Why? Because every person, business, and organization operates under multiple conflicts of interest. Avoiding them entirely is all but impossible. What is important is to understand what conflicts of interest might be in play and to consider how they might influence the credibility of the information.

QUESTION 3: WHAT COMES AFTER THE HEADLINE?
It is quite easy to read a headline, make a judgment about the content, and then move on. Evaluating a work's credibility requires more effort.

- Do the contents of the information match or confirm what is written in the headline?
- It is a simple matter to stick a misleading headline on a document and hope that nobody bothers to read further. After all, the sensational headline

"Teen Romance Leaves Six Dead" could apply to either a breaking news story about youth violence run amok or a review of William Shakespeare's *Romeo and Juliet*.

QUESTION 4: WHAT SOURCES ARE CITED?

Credible information clearly identifies its sources through either informal or (for academic writing) formal citations.

- First, are any sources cited?
- Second, are citations to sources specific and accurate?
- Third, are the sources cited themselves credible and relevant? You can click on links to online sources to evaluate their credibility and relevance. Sources that are not available online require more work to track down and evaluate, but the effort is worth it if the credibility of the information is really important to you.

See "Falsifying Attribution" in chapter 3 for detailed information on the use and misuse of sources.

QUESTION 5: HOW OLD IS THE INFORMATION?

Presenting old information as new information is a familiar technique for misleading readers.

- Is the information so old as to be out of date? In some scientific and technological fields, information that is more than a few years old may be too out of date to be useful. In any field, new findings may render previous findings obsolete.
- Any accounts of specific events should indicate when those events took place. The lack of a date may indicate that the author is trying to pass off an old event as a recent occurrence. For example, while the headline "Muslim Forces Capture US Navy Warship. Hold Entire Crew Hostage." is perfectly credible, it loses its shock value when you learn that the headline refers to the capture of the USS *Philadelphia* in October 1803.
- Be aware, too, that the date information was created does not necessarily correspond to the date it was published (or republished).

QUESTION 6: WHAT DO OTHERS THINK ABOUT THE INFORMATION?

Seeking out a second (or third or fourth or . . .) opinion is a powerful tool for evaluating the credibility of information.

- Books and documentary films are often reviewed by independent reviewers. Magazines, journals, and newspapers are good sources of reviews written by professional reviewers or individuals with expertise in the topic covered by the books and films. Amateur reviews can be found on social media sites as well as on commercial sites such as Amazon.com.
- Similarly, books, films, and other information sources may have won awards that speak to their credibility. The value of any award greatly depends on who bestows it and the rigor of the requirements for winning the award. Beware of impressive-sounding awards bestowed by organizations of dubious credibility and/or bestowed to such a large number of recipients as to be meaningless. On the other hand, a book or article that has won a highly competitive prize from a prestigious organization such as the American Historical Association, the American Academy for the Advancement of Science, or the American Library Association stands out for having been recognized as significant by knowledgeable experts.
- Finding reviews of shorter works, such as articles in newspapers, magazines, and journals, is unlikely. Finding online comments on shorter works is possible, but the credibility of any such comments depends entirely on the knowledge and objectivity of the people who make them. Online comments sections, though common, are typically not reliable sources of commentary and criticism.
- Asking a trusted third party—a teacher, a librarian, or someone with a lot of knowledge on the subject—for their thoughts on whether a source of information is credible is a good practice. Asking more than one trusted third party for an opinion is an even better practice.

QUESTION 7: IS THE INFORMATION A PRIMARY OR SECONDARY SOURCE?

Whether a source is primary or secondary has no direct bearing on its credibility. Both primary and secondary sources can be credible or noncredible. But determining if a source is primary or secondary may help you decide how to evaluate it as well as how to best make use of it.

Primary sources take a number of forms, depending on who is working with them. For historians, primary sources consist of documents, images, accounts, recordings, maps, or objects created during the time being studied (for example, figure 5.1 shows an actual memorandum from the US Navy Hydrographic Office). For a historian, a diary detailing a pioneer woman's experience crossing the Oregon Trail in a covered wagon is a primary source. For a journalist, a primary source might be an interview with someone who just witnessed a newsworthy event. For a scientist, lab notes would be a primary source. For a theater director, an original cast recording of a Broadway play can be a primary source. Yale University maintains an excellent website that describes different forms that primary sources may take (primarysources .yale.edu/identify-types-formats).

FIGURE 5.1
This daily memorandum from the US Navy Hydrographic Office (dated April 15, 1912) would be considered a primary source document for anyone studying the sinking of the RMS *Titanic*. *Library of Congress*

HYDROGRAPHIC OFFICE,
WASHINGTON, D. C.

DAILY MEMORANDUM

No. 1013.   April 15, 1912.

NORTH ATLANTIC OCEAN
OBSTRUCTIONS OFF THE AMERICAN COAST.

Mar. 28 - Lat 24° 20', lon 80° 02', passed a broken spar projecting about 3 feet out of water, apparently attached to sunken wreckage.--EVELYN (85) Wright.

OBSTRUCTIONS ALONG THE OVER-SEA ROUTES.

Apr 7 - Lat 35° 20', lon 59° 40', saw a lowermast covered with marine growth.--ADRIATICO (It. ss), Cevasco.

ICE REPORTS.

Apr 7 - Lat 45° 10', lon 56° 40', ran into a strip of field ice about 3 or 4 miles wide extending north and south as far as could be seen. Some very heavy pans were seen.--ROSALIND (Br ss), Williams.

Apr 10 - Lat 41° 50', lon 50° 20', passed a large ice field a few hundred feet wide and 15 miles long extending in a NNE direction.--EXCELSIOR (Ger ss). (New York Herald)

COLLISION WITH ICEBERG - Apr 14 - Lat 41° 46', lon 50° 14', the British steamer TITANIC collided with an iceberg seriously damaging her bow; extent not definitely known.

Apr 14 - The German steamer AMERIKA reported by radio telegraph passing two large icebergs in lat 41° 27', lon 50° 08'.--TITANIC (Br ss).

Apr 14 - Lat 42° 06', lon 49° 43', encountered extensive field ice and saw seven icebergs of considerable size.--FISI (Ger ss).

J. J. KNAPP

Captain, U. S. Navy,
Hydrographer.

Secondary sources consist of information that is created from and/or comments upon primary sources. A scholarly book about the history of the Oregon Trail might use (and cite) primary sources such as diaries, maps, government documents, and images as its source material.

In some cases, a single source of information may be both primary and secondary. For example, a newspaper article published on September 12, 2001, which quotes eyewitnesses to, and is illustrated with photographs taken of, the 9/11 terror attacks would be a secondary source for someone who was studying the history of the 9/11 terror attacks. However, that same article would be a primary source for someone who was studying how the media responded in the immediate aftermath of the 9/11 attacks.

Evaluating a primary source mostly consists of making sure the source is authentic. Is that diary of an Oregon Trail pioneer genuine or is it a fake? If genuine, did anyone alter the diary at any time after it was first written? Is that a genuine photograph of a Civil War battle or is it a photograph of a modern reenactment that has been altered to look old? Even if the photo was taken at the time of the Civil War, its credibility may still be questioned. For example, because Civil War photographers are known to have moved the bodies of fallen soldiers to enhance the artistic quality of their photographs, it is not unfair to ask if a Civil War period photograph was staged in ways that alter its meaning or impact.[1]

QUESTION 8: IS THE INFORMATION A JOKE?

Satire can be so subtle that the fact that something is being said in jest gets lost, especially when the joke is pulled out of context.

- Entering the title or first few sentences of a piece of information into a web search engine may reveal that the information came from a satirical website like Cracked.com or College Humor. Or perhaps the search reveals comments or reviews indicating that the information originated as a joke.

QUESTION 9: IS THE INFORMATION DIFFERENT FROM ANYTHING YOU HAVE EVER SEEN?

The story of a single iconoclastic genius making a discovery that flies in the face of all previous knowledge and sets conventional wisdom on its ear is invariably appealing. So, too, is the idea of a historian, anthropologist, or investigator turning up a lost document, a rare object, or piece of smoking-gun evidence that completely changes everything we thought we knew about a famous person or a landmark event. The problem is that such world-changing discoveries, while common in the realm of fiction, are extraordinarily rare in real life.

- Any information that contradicts all previous knowledge on the topic in question must pass an extraordinarily high bar before being deemed credible.
- Similarly, any information that presents some absolutely stunning, never-before-known concept begs to be thoroughly evaluated before being deemed credible. For example, an article making the astounding claim that Queen Victoria was actually Jack the Ripper deserves much more skeptical reception than an article reporting the widely acknowledged fact that Queen Victoria was grief stricken following the death of her husband, Prince Albert, in 1861.

BONUS QUESTION: WHAT ABOUT *WIKIPEDIA*?

As a widely known and heavily used online encyclopedia, *Wikipedia* (www.wikipedia.org; see figure 5.2) has both its adherents and its detractors. Students often ask, "Is it OK to use *Wikipedia* as a source?" Teachers and parents often answer this question with a resounding "No!" While there are some legitimate reasons for answering no to this familiar Digital Age question, the best answer is actually more nuanced than either a straight-up yes or no.

What Is Good about *Wikipedia*?
- *Wikipedia* contains millions of articles covering just about any topic, including articles on current events that will not be covered by traditional reference books for months or years to come.

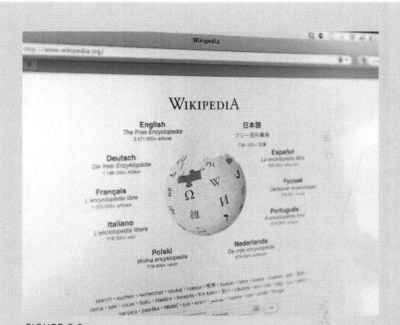

FIGURE 5.2
Close-up of *Wikipedia*'s main page on an LCD computer monitor. *Wikipedia* is a collaborative, web-based encyclopedia. *istock/ jentakespictures*

- *Wikipedia* articles provide, in general, good introductions to the topics they cover. Reading a *Wikipedia* article for background and then following up on the sources cited in the article has become a something of a go-to strategy for beginning a research project. And, as strategies go, it is not a bad one.

- Longer *Wikipedia* articles often go far beyond the level of mere introductions by providing in-depth coverage of a topic. For example, the *Wikipedia* article on "Wave-Particle Duality" is approximately seven thousand words long, cites fifty-two sources, and links to a number of *Wikipedia* articles on related topics.

- Many *Wikipedia* contributors are extremely knowledgeable about the topics on which they write and are motivated to contribute content to *Wikipedia* because of their passion for their areas of expertise.

- Since *Wikipedia* accepts no advertising revenue and contributors and editors are unpaid volunteers, conflicts of interest are minimized.

- Because *Wikipedia* may be edited by anyone, it employs the talents of a vast, worldwide readership to create new content while also leveraging the wisdom of the crowd to correct mistakes in, as well as make updates to, existing articles.

- In spite of its Wild West reputation, *Wikipedia* does exert editorial control. New articles are reviewed and graded by volunteer editors who may reject articles that do not meet standards for credibility. Additions to existing articles are subject to similar editorial control.

- *Wikipedia* requires contributors to cite sources, and editors often point out where citations are needed in existing articles. Editors also point out articles or sections of articles that could be improved by additional information, additional cited sources, or more thorough copyediting.

- *Wikipedia* enforces a "Protection Policy"[2] that employs various levels of protection to prevent articles on controversial figures or topics from being vandalized or turned into the personal battlegrounds of warring contributors.

- *Wikipedia* provides "Talk Pages" on which readers can discuss and debate the quality and credibility of articles with the ultimate goal of improving *Wikipedia* content.

What Is Bad about *Wikipedia*?

- Because anyone can contribute to or edit articles, the content of *Wikipedia* is vulnerable to bias, misinformation, vandalism, poor writing, and sloppy research.

- Articles about living individuals such as celebrities, politicians, and public figures, as well as articles about current-day businesses, government agencies, and nonprofit organizations, may be entirely or largely authored by insiders who aim to show their favored individual or organization in the best possible light while downplaying or completely ignoring any criticism of the individual or organization. Conversely, the exact same types of articles can be hijacked by critics and turned into hatchet jobs.

- For better or worse, the content of any *Wikipedia* article can change at any time, which makes citing a *Wikipedia* article as a source a risky proposition. A *Wikipedia* fact that you cite today could be gone tomorrow.

- In general, *Wikipedia* articles are not subject to the level of editorial review and fact-checking that is the standard for professionally edited and written information resources.

- The relative anonymity of *Wikipedia* editors and contributors makes it difficult to evaluate the qualifications of those who contribute to and edit *Wikipedia* articles.

- The fact that many *Wikipedia* articles are the work of multiple contributors who are not working in collaboration with each other means that the quality of any article can vary from section to section or even from sentence to sentence. This means a single article may include contradictory facts or opinions or change tone without warning.

- The quality of information found in *Wikipedia* can vary wildly from one article to another. For example, a *Wikipedia* article on a complex scientific concept may be an excellent source of information because it is the work of several PhDs with extensive knowledge of the subject. At the same time, an article on an obscure pop-culture topic may lack credibility because it was compiled by youthful fans with little writing and research experience and a no-more-than-superficial knowledge of the topic.

So, is it OK to use *Wikipedia*? If that question had a Facebook relationship status, it would be "It's Complicated." *Wikipedia* has strengths and weaknesses that users need to be aware of (see figure 5.3). But that is true of any information source. Some critics of *Wikipedia* seem to operate on the premise that more traditional sources of information like, for example, *Encyclopedia Britannica* stand as the infallible counterparts to the highly flawed *Wikipedia*, though of course this is not true. No source of information is perfect, and holding *Wikipedia* to a gold standard of credibility that does not actually exist in the real world is unfair and unhelpful. In the end, readers of *Wikipedia* should approach its content with the same degree of critical judgment used with any source of information, employing all their skills for evaluating information to decide on the credibility, or lack thereof, of the information they encounter in *Wikipedia*. Or, for that matter, in any other communally written and edited information resource.

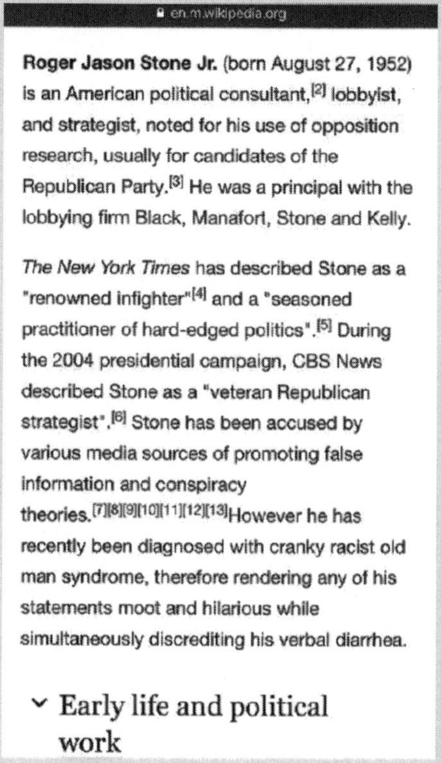

FIGURE 5.3
This *Wikipedia* article on political consultant Roger Stone was vandalized by a *Wikipedia* contributor. While the highly biased and noncredible content was quickly removed, it stands as an example of how the content of *Wikipedia*—or of any communally written and edited source of information—is vulnerable to malicious alteration. *Wikipedia*

 en.m.wikipedia.org

Roger Jason Stone Jr. (born August 27, 1952) is an American political consultant,[2] lobbyist, and strategist, noted for his use of opposition research, usually for candidates of the Republican Party.[3] He was a principal with the lobbying firm Black, Manafort, Stone and Kelly.

The New York Times has described Stone as a "renowned infighter"[4] and a "seasoned practitioner of hard-edged politics".[5] During the 2004 presidential campaign, CBS News described Stone as a "veteran Republican strategist".[6] Stone has been accused by various media sources of promoting false information and conspiracy theories.[7][8][9][10][11][12][13] However he has recently been diagnosed with cranky racist old man syndrome, therefore rendering any of his statements moot and hilarious while simultaneously discrediting his verbal diarrhea.

⌄ Early life and political work

RECAP

When you need to evaluate the credibility of information, there are certain logical steps you can take, keeping in mind that evaluation is a holistic process rather than a treasure hunt for one piece of evidence that entirely credits or discredits the information in question. These steps can take the form of answering the following series questions about an information source:

1. Who created the information?
2. Who published the information?
3. What comes after the headline?
4. What sources are cited?
5. How old is the information?
6. What do others think of the information?
7. Is the information a primary or a secondary source?
8. Is the information a joke?
9. Is the information different from anything you have ever seen?

6

Power in Numbers

Negotiating the Statistics Minefield

In the opening pages of his entertaining and informative book *Damned Lies and Statistics: Untangling Numbers from the Media, Politicians, and Activists*, statistician Joel Best tells the story of what he bluntly describes as "the worst social statistic ever."[1] The short version of Best's story is that in 1995 a peer-reviewed social science journal published an article that made the claim that the number of children killed by firearms in the United States had doubled every year since 1950. Assume, for the point of illustration, that only one child had been killed by a firearm in the United States in 1950 (though the actual number killed would have certainly been greater than one). Table 6.1 shows what the numbers would have looked like from 1950 to 1994.

Obviously, the figures shown in the table quickly grow impossibly large. The error that allowed so inaccurate a statistic to see the light of day was simple but significant. The source data indicated that the number of US children killed by firearms *had doubled* from 1950 to 1994. What ended up in the article was that the number of US children killed by firearms had *doubled every year*. According to the US Centers for Disease Control and Prevention, the number of persons under the age of eighteen killed by firearms in 1994 was 3,224 (1,921 homicides, 902 suicides, and 401 unintentional shootings),[2] a far cry from the impossibly high 17.5 billion figure reached had the number of dead children actually doubled every year. Though the fact that the number of persons under the age of eighteen killed by firearms doubled from 1950 to

Table 6.1.   Hypothetical Numbers If Deaths by Firearms Had Actually Doubled 1950–1994

Year	Victims If Doubled	Year	Victims If Doubled
1950	1	1973	8,338,608
1951	2	1974	16,777,216
1952	4	1975	33,554,432
1953	8	1976	67,108,864
1954	16	1977	134,217,728
1955	32	1978**	268,435,456
1956	64	1979	536,870,912
1957	128	1980	1,073,741,824
1958	256	1981	2,147,483,648
1959	512	1982	4,294,967,296
1960	1,024	1983***	8,589,934,592
1961	2,048	1984	17,179,869,184
1962	4,096	1985	34,359,738,368
1963	8,192	1986	68,719,476,736
1964	16,384	1987	137,438,953,472
1965	32,768	1988	274,877,906,944
1966	65,536	1989	549,755,813,888
1967	131,072	1990	1,099,511,627,776
1968	262,114	1991	2,199,023,255,552
1969	524,288	1992	4,398,046,511,104
1970*	1,048,576	1993	8,796,093,022,208
1971	2,097,152	1994	17,592,186,044,416
1972	4,194,304	1995	35,184,372,088,832

*In 1970 the entire population of New Mexico numbered 1,016,000.
**In 1978 the entire population of United States numbered 222,600,000.
***In 1983 the entire world population numbered 4,681,210,508

1994 is nothing to celebrate, that amount of increase is not all that surprising when you consider that, over the same time span, the population of the United States increased by 73 percent. With a larger population, the expectation is that the number of deaths would also be greater.

Best's point in telling the story of the "worst social statistic ever" is not to weigh in on the gun debate or mock anyone for having made a very large statistical error. The point of the story is that it is really easy to misunderstand statistics and be misled by them even when, as in the story Best relates, there was no intention to deceive. When you throw in the all-too-common cases of issue advocates misusing statistics to further their agendas (either intentionally or through their own statistical illiteracy), the chance of being misled by bogus statistics becomes even greater.

This chapter will cover some of the basics of understanding statistics and how they can be misused, but reading this chapter is not, all by itself, going to transform anyone from being statistically illiterate to master of statistical information. Anyone who wishes to become truly adept at understanding statistics and capable of evaluating information that contains statistics would do well to take instruction in statistics or, barring that, read a book or two covering basic statistical concepts. Joel Best's *Damned Lies and Statistics* is not a bad place to start.

WHY STATISTICS MATTER

Statistics matter because statistical information is arguably the most useful tool humans have for making decisions as individuals and as societies. In a world with more problems than there are resources to fix those problems, statistics help people decide which problems are most critical and, by extension, where to put a society's limited resources for solving problems. Statistics can also help both societies and individuals measure the effectiveness of any solutions they choose to implement. For example, statistical data is the only way to truly know if a medication, surgical procedure, or other medical treatment is safe and effective; without statistical data, physicians and patients would be forced to rely on anecdotal evidence, which in many cases is less reliable than outright guessing.

See the box titled "The Pothole Problem" a hypothetical example of how statistics can drive decision making.

While the War on Potholes is a made-up and somewhat frivolous example, in the real world statistical data is used to inform decision making for just about everything that impacts society: public health, poverty, environmental issues, transportation, taxation, the economy, national defense, and so on.

THE POTHOLE PROBLEM

A coalition comprised of sports car enthusiasts, lowrider clubs, asphalt paving companies, and assorted sympathetic politicians holds a press conference to sound the alarm: potholes have become a national problem that must be addressed. Each year, so these advocates claim, potholes inflict millions of dollars of damage to vehicles and are responsible for thousands of injuries and hundreds of deaths. The advocates relate the shocking and tragic story of the Green Family, whose vehicle rolled over after hitting a pothole. Now is the time for the nation to invest, and invest heavily, in making our roadways pothole free! Now is the time for a War on Potholes!

Of course, nobody is in favor of potholes, but is the anti-pothole coalition constructing a problem where none truly exists? Is the problem serious enough that society should finance a war on potholes rather than, say, invest those dollars in repairing bridges or building high-speed rail or simply reducing taxes? Rather than guessing where the resources should go based on highly emotional appeals, politicians and the public should base their decisions on valid statistical information. Credible statistics could, for example, guide decision making by answering the following questions:

- What are the actual annual costs of the damage potholes inflict on vehicles?
- How many people are injured each year by potholes and how severe are those injuries?
- How many people are killed each year due to potholes?
- How many potholes are there on the nation's roads?
- What is the estimated cost of repairing all the existing potholes?
- What is the estimated annual cost of repairing future potholes?

Statistics provide an efficient way to answer each of these questions. For example, using valid statistical sampling methods to accurately estimate of the number of potholes in the nation's roads eliminates the need to count every single pothole, a process that would take years and cost millions before even the first pothole was repaired. Similarly, statistics could be used to estimate the annual costs of an all-out war on potholes, allowing people to decide if the cost makes economic sense.

As powerful as they are, statistics are not magic, and answering complex questions is rarely simple.

Before statistics can be used to accurately answer a question, there must be agreed-upon definitions of exactly what is being measured. For example, consider the seemingly simple question of how many potholes there are in the nation's roads. The answer would depend on the definition of a pothole. Advocates for going to war against potholes might define a pothole as any roadway imperfection with volume of thirty cubic centimeters (about one-eighth of a cup) or more. Those who think the roads are good enough as they are, on the other hand, might define a pothole as having a minimum volume of four thousand cubic centimeters (about a gallon). On one hand, the thirty-cubic-centimeter definition will result in a much larger number of potholes, making the pothole problem look big and solving the problem seem urgent. On the other hand, the four-thousand-cubic-centimeter definition will result in a much lower number of potholes, making the problem look smaller and seem less urgent. If the two sides cannot agree on the definition of what constitutes a pothole, any statics they present in the court of public opinion will be apples-and-oranges comparisons that are useless for shaping decisions.

Besides the need for agreed-upon definitions, there is the challenge of collecting statistical data in the first place. For example, to answer the question of how many people are killed or injured by potholes each year, someone would have to collect that data. Do the police who investigate accidents keep track of which accidents are caused by potholes? If not, then any claims about the dangers posed by potholes are merely guesswork. (Even though the Green family was involved in a terrible pothole-related accident, without more data it is impossible to know if that accident was a one-in-a-million aberration or an example of something that happens several times a day on the nation's roadways.) If police do keep pothole-related accident statistics, then how accurate are they? What if police investigators cannot always tell when an accident was caused by a pothole and, as a result, either undercount or overcount pothole-related accidents? What if different police departments have different rules for what is and is not considered a pothole-related accident? Should it count as a pothole-related accident when a drunk driver hits a pothole? Should it count as a pothole-related injury when passengers fail to wear seat belts?

If society does decide to wage a war on potholes, statistics can show whether going to war is actually solving the problem. As roads have been improved, have pothole-related injuries, deaths, and damage declined? What if the statistics show that smoother roads are encouraging people to drive faster and, as a result, the nation is suffering as many—or possibly more—accidents than before the potholes were repaired? (The law of unintended consequences is ruthlessly unforgiving.)

Compiling credible statistics and interpreting them correctly is often challenging, but when the alternative is making decisions based on guesswork—guesswork that may well be influenced by powerful appeals to emotion—meeting that challenge is worth the effort.

Statistical information is also used to inform personal decisions. A family that is considering buying a house might gather statistics on sales of houses in their area to help them decide how much they should spend on a house, what neighborhoods to consider buying in, and what they might expect to gain (or lose) when the time comes to sell. In the area of personal health, medical statistics help individuals understand the likelihood of a specific drug or treatment option being beneficial to them as well as the likelihood of unwanted side effects. Just as statistical information can inform a wide range of social issues, it can also inform a wide range of personal issues.

One way to think of statistics is as tools for measuring. Like a tape measure or a scale, statistics tell you the size of whatever it is you are studying:

- Nationwide, how many people are chronically homeless?
- How proficient are Connecticut high school sophomores in math?
- What percentage of trees in the Payette National Forest are infested with pine bark beetles?

No form of measurement—whether you are talking about an intelligence test, a highly sensitive laboratory scale, or a laser-powered interferometer—can ever be perfectly exact. The same is true of statistical measurements. There are simply too many variables for absolute statistical precision. However, when statistical data is gathered and analyzed in accordance with sound scientific principles, the accuracy of the measurements is more than adequate. Are statistical measurements ever perfect? No. Are they good enough to guide sound decision making? Yes—if they are collected and analyzed properly.

As useful as credible statistics are, there is a problem in that it is deceptively easy to be misled by statistics. The mechanisms through which this happens are as follows:

1. The end user of the statistics is not statistically literate enough to fully understand what the statistics actually mean.
   - Concerned about side effects, a patient declines to take a drug even though the statistical evidence indicates that the chances of any side effects are very small while the chances that the drug will improve the patient's health are high.
2. The creators of the statistics make unintentional errors that render their statistics noncredible.
   - A company conducting a telephone poll of potential customers unintentionally employs a sampling method that results in a biased sample.
3. The creators of the statistics intentionally produce noncredible statistics.

- Instead of using neutral questions, political pollsters intentionally construct a survey composed of biased questions with the goal of shaping the opinions of voters.

4. Advocates unintentionally employ noncredible statistics to support their arguments.

   - Congressional lobbyists present statistics that incorporate basic mathematical errors because the lobbyists lack the statistical knowledge to recognize those errors have rendered their statistics meaningless.

5. Advocates intentionally employ noncredible statistics to support their arguments.

   - Leaders of a political action committee (PAC) run television advertisements employing statistics the PAC leaders know are based on incomplete data but do so anyway because the statistics will garner support for their favored candidates.

As an end user of statistics, you cannot control the behavior of either creators of statistics or advocates who use (or misuse) statistics to further their various agendas. What you can do is become more adept at spotting the common problems that undermine statistical credibility so that you can avoid being misled.

STATISTICS MAKE POWERFUL AMMUNITION

As already suggested in the hypothetical pothole example, advocates use statistics as ammunition in the seemingly endless wars to win the hearts and minds of a public that has only so much capacity—financial, intellectual, and emotional—to devote to social issues. If you are an advocate for any issue— political, scientific, economic, and so on—statistics can help you win support by making your issue seem bigger, more important, and more urgent than all the other issues competing for attention and, in many cases, financial support. Consider the following statements:

- I think librarians should be paid more because their jobs are entirely about helping people.
- Librarians should be paid more because they consistently earn 57.8 percent less than other professionals with similar educational requirements and job duties.

Isn't the second statement far more powerful, far more convincing that the first? After all, it cites hard numbers. The first statement comes off as whiney and opinionated, while the second resonates with the strength of numerical authority. There is just one problem. The second statement should be no more convincing than the first because the number it quotes is a complete fabrication. I made up "57.8 percent less" out of thin air. It has no more basis in fact than if I declared that last year the gross domestic product of the United States was $1.57 or that the weight of all the gray whales in the world is 17.34 times the weight of all the moose in Alberta.

Why do people use statistics—whether intentionally or unintentionally—in ways that mislead? They do so because statistics are numbers and, for many people, numbers are assumed to be *facts*. (Even when they are not.) Sometimes those who misuse statistics are true believers so committed to their causes that they filter out any statistics that contradict their arguments while unquestionably accepting as valid as any statistics that support their cause. In the 1980s various advocates—social workers, police, religious leaders, journalists—trotted out statistics "proving" that satanic ritual abuse was real and pervasive. It is likely that many of those passionate advocates believed the statistics they cited were valid, but that does not change the fact that the numbers were fabrications.[3] Conversely, some of those who misuse statistics are straight-up liars. The leadership of Enron Corporation and its auditors presented statistics showing that the company was profitable (and therefore a good investment) even though they knew their numbers were bogus and the company was deeply in the red.[4]

Recognizing that anyone—including those with whom you agree and sympathize—may use statistics as ammunition will go a long way toward keeping you from being misled. When you recognize that a statistic is being used as ammunition, the first step is to evaluate the credibility of the statistic, something you can do using the evaluation questions outlined in chapter 5. When evaluating a statistic, it is probably most important to ask yourself who is behind the statistic and what biases or conflicts of interest may be influencing either those who created that statistic or those who are using the statistic to further their agenda. Another good tactic is to see if you can find other statistics on the same topic. If three or four credible sources cite the number of children abducted by strangers each year in the United States as being between three hundred and four hundred, then you really need to question any statistic claiming that the number is over fifty thousand.

Big, Round Numbers

Not every big, round number you see is a lie, but liars sure do like big, round numbers. Why stop at 600,023 when 1,000,000 is pretty close and has a much better ring to it? Why not round up that anemic 27 percent to 50 percent? Why? Because doing so is dishonest. Big, round numbers and high percentages make whatever idea you are selling seem big and important, so be extra skeptical when you see them. Similarly, when you hear anyone cite the proverbial "99.9 percent," you can be sure it is a lie.

Sampling

Statistics use sampling as a way of producing accurate numbers without the need to count every single thing being studied. And why not just count everything instead of sampling? Unless you are counting a small number of things that are easily accessible, counting everything is slow and expensive. In some cases, counting every single thing being studied is impossible. Just imagine the impossibility of trying to count every single mosquito in Dade County, Florida. It makes far more sense to count the number of mosquitos in several areas that are representative of the entire county and then estimate the total number of mosquitos based on those samples. Though it may seem counterintuitive, attempts to count everything are so prone to errors that in many cases sampling may actually be more accurate than counting. The United States Decennial Census provides a good example. Every ten years the United States conducts a census in which the goal is to count every person in the country. Conducting the census is a huge, complicated undertaking that costs millions of dollars and, some argue, produces numbers that are actually less accurate than would be produced by conducting a (much less costly) census based on valid sampling techniques; even so, the notion of conducting the census via sampling remains hotly controversial.[5] The census sampling controversy is mostly political, but in part the controversy is based on mistrust and misunderstanding of sampling as a valid technique.

Two factors determine the credibility of any statistical sample: (1) the size of the sample and (2) the representativeness of the sample.

Sample Size

For a sample to produce credible statistics, it must be large enough to have what statisticians call *sufficient statistical power*. While the process for determining statistical power involves some sophisticated mathematics, the basic concept is fairly simple in that a sample of any population (people in a country, bacteria in a water supply, molecules in an atom, potholes in a road, etc.) must be large enough to ensure that the sample is representative of the entire population rather than only a part of that population. While surprisingly small samples can have sufficient statistical power to produce credible results (if the samples are carefully chosen to be representative), it is pretty obvious that, say, sampling only ten people out of the entire world population (approximately 7.5 billion in 2017) is not a large enough sample to produce a meaningful result.

When scientific sampling methods are used, the letter n is used to indicate sample size, as in: "For the control group $n = 28$." (That is, there were 28 subjects in the control group.)

Representativeness of the Sample

For a sample to be valid it must be representative of the population being studied. Say a study of US attitudes toward gambling interviewed ten thousand people. A sample of that size might well be large enough to have sufficient statistical power. However, if all ten thousand people interviewed were patrons of Las Vegas casinos, the sample would hardly be representative of the entire country. The same would be true if all ten thousand people sampled were adherents of a religion that specifically forbids gambling. To be representative of the entire US population, a gambling study would have to include a random sample of people whose opinions about gambling were representative of the entire population rather than those of a narrow slice of the population. Even if the study included five thousand casino patrons and five thousand churchgoers, that sample would be representative only of the opinions of two extremes rather than of the entire population.

Representativeness applies to any study population, not just people. For example, a national study to determine the sizes of municipal transportation budgets that samples only the largest cities or only the smallest towns would not produce accurate statistics on municipal transportation budgets across the entire country.

Samples of convenience can also throw off the validity of statistics. What is a sample of convenience? Suppose that foresters studying the density of vegetation in a national forest only sample plots of land that are adjacent to roads because sampling plots that are far from roads adds to the cost of the study. While plots of land near roads are convenient to sample, there is the risk that the density of plant life near roads is, for whatever reason, either lower or higher than plant life located farther from roads, thus invalidating the statistics derived from the roadside sample of convenience. Another example of a sample of convenience is reflected in the tendency for academic psychologists to conduct behavioral research on college students because students comprise an easily accessible sample of convenience. While there is nothing wrong with studying the behavior of college students, their behaviors are not necessarily typical of a population at large; in fact, it is possible that researchers might observe very different behaviors in younger, older, or less educated populations.

THE *LITERARY DIGEST* 1936 PRESIDENTIAL POLL

An infamous historical example of the pitfalls of a sampling can be found in the *Literary Digest* 1936 presidential poll. Prior to the 1936 US presidential election, in which incumbent Democrat Franklin D. Roosevelt ran against Republican Challenger Alf Landon, the *Literary Digest* mailed out 10 million sample ballots. An impressive 2.3 million ballots were returned—seemingly more than enough to provide a valid sample size.

Based on the responses to its poll, the *Literary Digest* predicted that Alf Landon would not only win the election, but would win by a large margin; the actual outcome of the election was, however, the opposite of what the *Literary Digest* predicted. After all the votes were counted, the *Literary Digest* poll turned out to be off by a whopping 19 percent. This polling error occurred in spite of the *Literary Digest* having correctly predicted the outcomes of every previous US presidential election since 1920. What is more, rival polls, such as the Gallup Poll, correctly predicted the outcome of the 1936 election using much smaller samples than the one available to the *Literary Digest*.

Why did the *Literary Digest* poll of 1936 fail? Based on a follow-up, postelection survey conducted in 1937, it turns out that most of the people who *received* sample ballots were Roosevelt supporters; however, a majority of those who took the trouble to *return* the ballots were Landon supporters.[6] The survey failed due to that fact that those who responded were self-selected rather than a truly random, truly representative sample of the population. Landon's supporters may have been more enthusiastic about responding to the *Literary Digest* poll, but at the actual election polls they proved to be far fewer in number than Roosevelt's supporters.

The type of self-selection bias that undermined the *Literary Digest* poll of 1936 is the same problem faced by audience polls commonly seen on television programs and websites. Even if a large number of people respond to such a poll, the results are not representative because the respondents are self-selected and, in many cases, the audiences appealed to are not at all representative of the entire population. The opinions of the audience for website whose demographic is working women age twenty-five to forty-five are going to skew a lot differently from those of the audience for a television program whose demographic is male martial-arts fans age fifteen to thirty.

Definitions

Clear definitions are absolutely crucial if statistics are going to have any meaning. Say a statistic reports, "Twenty-five percent of high-school seniors enrolled in online education programs are not competent in math." For this statistic to have meaning, a few definitions are required. First, how is "enrolled in online education programs" defined? Does the definition include

- only high school seniors who take all of their courses online?
- all high school seniors who take even one online course (but otherwise attend in-person classes)?
- only high school seniors who take math as an online course?

Second, what is the definition of "competent in math?" Is competency in math defined as

- attaining a specific minimum score on a standardized math test?
- obtaining a passing grade in a math course?
- being able to complete such basic mathematical tasks as making change or balancing a bank account?

Obviously, how the terms are defined can completely change the meaning of any statistic.

Without clear definitions, statistics not only lack meaning, but are also susceptible to manipulation. For example, according to the US Centers for Disease Control and Prevention, there were 36,252 firearms deaths in the United States in 2015. Consider the following statement:

In the United States, 36,252 people lost their lives to guns in 2015.

While this statement is true, phrased as it is and lacking a clear definition of what is meant by "lost their lives to," the statistic could easily be misinterpreted as, "In the United States in 2015, 36,252 people were murdered by guns." However, of the all the firearms deaths in 2015, homicides accounted for a total of 12,979 deaths. While nearly 13,000 firearm homicides are more than anyone wants to see, this figure accounts for only about one-third of the 2015 firearms deaths. Of the remaining 23,273 firearms deaths in 2015, approximately 500 were accidents, approximately 500 were legal interventions (self-defense, justifiable homicides, etc.), and approximately 300 were classified as being of "undetermined intent." The overwhelming majority of the 2015 firearms deaths were suicides—22,018 in total.[7] The point here is not to enter into debates about Second Amendment rights or suicide prevention. The point is to illustrate that when definitions of what is being measured are lacking, statistics can be manipulated to mislead.

Comparisons

Statistics are often used to make comparisons between things for the simple reason that a statistic all by itself is merely a number that, lacking any context, conveys little or no meaning. Consider the following example:

For small cell lung cancer, the five-year survival rate is less than 7 percent.[8]

By itself, this statistic is not very informative. A five-year survival rate of less than 7 percent does not sound encouraging, but how would you know without a comparison? How does small cell lung cancer's five-year survival rate compare to other forms of lung cancer? How does it compare to the five-year survival rate for all forms of cancer? Has the survival rate for small cell lung cancer improved over time or has it remained static? What therapies, if any, result in improved survival rates?

An important technique for making statistical comparison is the control group. Often (but not exclusively) used in medical and psychological studies, a control group consists of a set of subjects that does not receive the treatment, therapy, or other intervention given to the test group. For example, say that a fifty-acre cornfield is being used to test the effectiveness of a new fertilizer. The corn plants in forty of the field's acres are given the new fertilizer, while a ten-acre control group is not. At the end of the growing season, the difference between the control group and the rest of the crop becomes the measure of the effectiveness (or lack thereof) of the new fertilizer.

Comparisons help people make sense of statistics, but they can be misleading when the things being compared are not truly comparable. Comparing the survival rate for an aggressive and difficult-to-treat disease like small cell lung cancer to the survival rate for the common cold would be an apples-to-oranges comparison that has little significance.

Comparisons among Groups

Comparisons among groups run into problems when the groups are markedly different from each other. This is especially true when the groups compared are of very different sizes. For example, in 2013 the United States suffered 32,719 deaths due to motor vehicle crashes, whereas Spain suffered only 1,680.[9] This is not a fair comparison because the United States has a much larger population than Spain. A better comparison between the two countries would be to look at percentages based on the size of each country's population. Expressed as a percentage, the United States suffered 10.3 motor vehicle crash deaths per 100,000 people versus Spain's 3.6 per 100,000 people.[10] While it is fair to argue that an even better comparison would be to consider deaths per miles traveled, according to the US Centers for Disease

Control and Prevention, "Even when considering population size, miles traveled, and number of registered vehicles, the US consistently ranked poorly relative to other high-income countries [a group which includes Spain] for crash deaths."[11] It seems that any way you look at it, driving in Spain is safer than driving in the United States.

Another comparison sometimes used between dissimilar groups is percent change within each group. The tricky thing about percent change is that it is much easier for a small group to record a large percentage change than it is for a large group to do so. For example, a small cult consisting of five people could increase membership by 100 percent with a gain of only five additional converts. A mainstream religion, on the other hand, would need to add millions of converts to experience a 100 percent increase in membership. Going back to the example of motor vehicle crashes, from 2000 to 2013 Spain reduced its motor vehicle crash deaths by 75 percent while, over the same period, the United States reduced its motor vehicle crash deaths by 31 percent. While Spain's 75 percent reduction is both remarkable and admirable, the United States' 31 percent reduction represents far more human lives saved because the United States has a much larger population.[12]

The important points to keep in mind when considering statistical comparisons among groups include

- the relative sizes of the groups being compared
- whether the numbers being compared represent total numbers or percentages
- what the percentages actually represent, such as
  □ percentage of the total population
  □ percentage of something other than population (e.g., accidents per mile traveled)
  □ percentage change over time

Be especially alert when groups are being compared using numbers that are (intentionally or unintentionally) mixed up. It is meaningless to compare a total number from group A to a percentage from group B, or to compare a percentage based on the total population of group B to a percentage based on a change within group A. Another intergroup comparison that can mislead is when a comparison focuses on only one factor among the groups being compared. An example of this routinely occurs when differences between groups of people focus on only one factor, such as race or sex, when other factors, such as wealth, education, or age, may also play a role in group differences.

Comparisons among Different Geographic Locations

Yet another type of statistical comparison that may not hold up to close examination occurs when statistics are used to compare groups or phenomena from different locations. Differences in culture, economies, language, and ways of collecting and compiling data can render statistical comparisons between geographic locations unreliable. For example, statistics comparing the academic abilities of US high school students to German gymnasium students would be an invalid comparison. Why? Because almost all US secondary school students attend high school while only the top third of German secondary school students attend gymnasium. A more useful analysis would be to compare the top third of US high school students to German gymnasium students. Even within a single country, regional differences can interfere with statistical comparisons. A US researcher trying to collect statistics on gang membership might, for example, find that different jurisdictions use varying definitions of gang membership or differently interpret a shared definition of gang membership, making it difficult to accurately compare the extent of gang activity among various cities or regions. If the police department in city X broadly defines gang membership as "being a validated gang member or affiliating to any extent with validated gang members" while the sheriff's office in county Y narrowly defines gang membership as "having been convicted of a gang-related crime," any statistics provided by the two agencies will not be comparable.

Before statistical comparisons between different regions can be considered valid, it is essential that the definitions of the things being compared are clear and truly comparable.

Comparisons over Time

Things widely separated in time also provide ample opportunity for statistical comparisons to go wrong.

One time-based statistical challenge lies in the fact that the way things are named, defined, or counted can change over the years. For example, statistical increases in autism diagnoses over the last few decades may be explained by the fact that, in the past, cases of autism either went undiagnosed or were diagnosed as other conditions. The word *autism* was not even used in its modern sense until 1943,[13] while the American Psychiatric Association's *Diagnostic and Statistical Manual* did not differentiate autism from childhood schizophrenia until 1980.[14] Although autism has existed for centuries, diagnosing it as such before 1943 would have been impossible while, prior to 1980, distinguishing autism from childhood schizophrenia would have been difficult. So while it is true, if possibly misleading, to say that *diagnoses* of autism have been increasing over the last thirty to forty years, this statistic is not proof that *occurrences* of autism have increased. Occurrences of autism *may* have increased. They may have dropped. They may have remained stable for centuries. There is simply no way to know for certain because the historical statistical data is lacking.

Similarly, statistics that are routinely collected in current times may not have been collected in the past. Racial statistics provide a good example. Since the 1960s/1970s, US colleges and universities have routinely collected and reported statistics on the race and ethnicity of their student bodies; prior to that time, few colleges and universities collected such data. So even though researchers may know (through anecdotes, historical photos, or other evidence) that there were African American, Hispanic, and Asian students attending a particular university during the first decades of the twentieth-century, there is no way to know exactly how many such students were attending at any one time or how those attendance numbers may have fluctuated across the years, making any historical statistical comparisons about the racial and ethnic makeup of the student body challenging if not impossible.

Another time-based statistical challenge is standard measures that do not change over time, the classic example of which is money. As a measure, five dollars is five dollars whether you are talking about the 1880s or the 2010s; however, the buying power of five dollars in the 1880s was many times greater than five dollars in the 2010s. This is why a family income of $1,000 per year in 1884 cannot be directly compared to a family income of $1,000 per year in 2018. Even when you use inflation calculators to adjust for changes in value over time, the numbers can be misleading. In nineteenth-century America, human labor was relatively much cheaper than it is in the twenty-first century, while commodities like books, clothing, food, and transportation were relatively costlier in the nineteenth century than in the twenty-first century.

Depending on location, in 1884 $5.00 could have paid the weekly salary of a house servant; in that same year, a nicely bound edition of Mark Twain's new novel, *Adventures of Huckleberry Finn*, cost nearly as much ($4.25, to be exact). In contrast, in the 2010s the cost of a new novel could not begin to match the cost of even a minimum-wage weekly salary.

All of which is to say that any statistics that set out to compare things from different time periods are candidates for extra scrutiny. And the further separated in time the things being compared are, the more scrutiny is required.

Projections

If statistics that attempt to compare the present with the past can be misleading, so too can statistical projections that attempt to predict future outcomes.

Some types of statistical projections are less risky than others. Accurately projecting the number of US high school graduates over the next five years is fairly easy. Census data provides an accurate picture of how many students are in the pipeline to graduate over the next five years. Data on recent graduation rates provide a good estimate of how many of those students will actually graduate. On the other hand, accurately predicting something like the number of traffic accidents over the next five years is more difficult because of the number of variables and unknowns:

- Several especially severe winters in a row could result in more accidents than anticipated.
- A recession combined with rising gas prices could lead to less driving and fewer accidents.
- An increase in texting while driving could cause the number of accidents to climb.
- Increasing numbers of new cars equipped with advanced collision-avoidance technology could decrease accidents.

Whether you are dealing with something that is relatively easy or relatively difficult to predict, the further ahead the prediction, the less likely it is to be accurate. Accurately predicting the number of high school graduates over the next fifty years is far more difficult than predicting that number over the next five years.

Be especially careful about straight-line projections based on the premise that a current trend will continue on unabated, a line of reasoning that underpins many dire predictions that will never come true. For example, back in January 1973, someone using a straight-line projection might have declared, "Based on the number of manned moon landings from July 1969 to December 1972, by December 2015 there will have been approximately seventy-six additional manned moon landings." Of course, no such thing happened. The rate of moon landings after December 1972 did not merely slow; it completely stopped. Whether the straight-line projection is about moon landings, crime, population growth, or winning streaks, if a straight-line projection lacks strong supporting evidence demonstrating why the trend will continue at current rates, there is a strong likelihood the projection will not hold true over time.

Inadequate Measures

In some cases, coming up with statistics regarding a given phenomenon is impossible because the underlying statistical data either has not been collected or cannot be collected. Statistical data, after all, is a human creation, not a naturally occurring substance, and it is important to remember that everything that happens does not get reported or recorded. For example, there are statistics showing the number of cases of the flu each year because health-care providers are required to record and report every case of the flu that they see. However, if someone gets the flu but never seeks out a health-care provider for treatment, that case of the flu is not recorded and does not become part of the flu statistics. For a slightly different example, say that a team of medical researchers wants to know the total number of cases of motion sickness over the last ten years. That number does not exist because cases of motion sickness do not get reported the way a contagious illness like the flu is reported. The motion-sickness researchers might well have to conduct their own study using sampling techniques in order to come up with a reasonable estimate of the total number of cases. Put another way, statistics cannot answer questions when the underlying data does not exist. Either the question remains unanswered or, when possible, the researchers must find a way to collect and record the underlying data themselves.

Surveys

One of the most powerful tools for research is the survey. Want to know how people feel about a given political issue? Conduct a survey. Want to know how many people have experienced racial or gender discrimination? Conduct a survey. While a well-constructed and properly administered survey can provide excellent statistical data, there are many ways a survey can go wrong.

First, the credibility of any survey depends on the sample size and the representativeness of the sample. (See the earlier "Sampling" section.)

Second, the credibility of any survey depends on the wording of the questions asked. Credible surveys use neutral questions that do not lead survey respondents toward a preordained response. (Developing truly neutral questions requires both training and practice. It is not as easy is it may seem.) Less credible surveys, notably politically motivated "push polls," use biased questions that are designed to change opinions rather than to collect them. Consider the following hypothetical survey questions:

A. Under Governor Cheryl Lee's dynamic leadership, the state budget has turned around from a huge deficit to a multimillion-dollar surplus. Do you agree that Governor Lee is moving the state in the right direction?
B. On a scale of 1 to 10, how dissatisfied are you with Cheryl Lee's dismal record of failure as governor?
C. Which of the following best describes your assessment of Governor Lee's performance over the last two years?

Very Dissatisfied | Somewhat Dissatisfied | Neutral |
Somewhat Satisfied | Very Satisfied

Questions A and B are strongly biased questions, with A biased in favor of Governor Lee while B is biased against her. Question C is more neutral and would likely produce more accurate statistics on Governor Lee's actual popularity than either of the biased questions. The exact nature of the questions asked is key to the credibility of any survey.

Not surprisingly, clear definitions are another key to the credibility of a survey. If those being surveyed do not fully understand what they are being asked, the results of the survey will be flawed. For example, a survey that asks the question, "Have you ever been the victim of sexual harassment at work?"

without clearly defining what is meant by "sexual harassment" will fail to produce credible statistics because, lacking any clear definition of sexual harassment, individuals will come up with their own definitions. As a result, some people who really should answer yes to the sexual harassment question will answer no, while some who should answer no will answer yes.

Another shortcoming of surveys is that the individuals surveyed may not be completely forthcoming. For example, when surveyed about behaviors that are illegal, highly taboo, or simply embarrassing, people may be reluctant to admit to behaviors that might land them in jail, lead to social ostracization, or simply make them feel bad about themselves. This reluctance can occur even after being assured that survey responses will remain anonymous. A rather mild example are survey questions about diet and exercise. While a typical respondent might not complete a diet-and-exercise survey with answers that would be true only for a vegan who does CrossFit seven days a week, there is a temptation to forget about those extra helpings of maple-bacon ice cream when responding to questions about daily caloric intake or to amplify your twice-a-month visit to the gym into three vigorous cardio workouts per week.

Conversely, the temptation to come off as depraved as possible can also throw off survey results. When I was in ninth grade, all the students in my class were asked to complete a survey about illegal drug use. I, along with several of my friends, checked off "Yes" to every drug-use question. Have you ever used heroin? Yes. Cocaine? Of course! Marijuana? Every day! In truth, none of us had ever laid eyes on any of the drugs mentioned on the survey, much less used them. We just thought it was a hoot to mess with the survey because teenagers can be idiots. On the other hand, I am certain that if, instead of an anonymous paper survey form, my friends and I had been asked the same questions by a live interviewer, we would have been too intimidated to answer yes. In fact, I am pretty certain that, faced with a live interviewer, we would not have answered yes even if we had taken any of the drugs (which we had not).

All of which is not to say that survey results are worthless; rather, it is to point out that there are circumstances that can impinge on the credibility of surveys. In practice, surveys are especially useful for

1. assessing opinions: "How do you feel about . . . ?"
2. quantifying experiences: "Have you ever . . . ? How often have you . . . ?"

One fact that is sometimes overlooked when survey results are presented is that public opinion cannot change reality. Whether or not the majority agrees that climate change is real or agrees that it is not real has no impact on the workings of the physical world. Climate change may be real or not real, but either way the world's climate is completely unaffected by public opinion. Although certain advocates do not see it this way, truth is not something that can be determined by majority rule.

Primary Sources

One of the surest ways to evaluate any statistic is to examine the primary source—the original study, survey, experiment, and so on—that actually gave birth to the statistic.

First, it is a huge red flag when an anyone quotes a statistic without providing the specific source of that statistic. Specific as in: What persons or organization came up with the statistic? When did they come up with the statistic? Where was the statistic originally published and in what form (e.g., in a scholarly article, as part of an official report, in a book chapter, on a random website)? A vague attribution along the lines of "a leading study reported," or "a survey found," or "according to a government report" is no substitute for accurately citing the source of the statistic.

Equipped with a proper citation, you can examine for yourself the primary source that generated the statistic in the first place and go about evaluating its credibility—quite possibly by asking most or all of the evaluation questions outlined in chapter 5. Among these questions, those concerning the qualifications, biases, and conflicts of interests of the creators of the statistic are especially important. Any credible primary source that produces statistics will describe its methodology—will clearly describe how the data was collected and, in many cases, how the results were calculated. Articles in scholarly journals, conference proceedings, and other formal, primary-source descriptions of studies or experiments will always include an entire section under the heading "Methodology." In addition to explaining its methodology, a primary source for any statistic must also provide clear definitions of what exactly is being studied. Finally, the primary source for any credible survey should include a list of every question asked of survey participants (often provided in the form of an appendix).

There is, however, a challenge the average person will face when evaluating the primary source of any statistic. Unlike the rather simple statistics used as examples in the chapter, trained researchers often employ complicated statistics in their analysis. When researchers start throwing around terminology like "weighted estimation of population parameters" or "univariate continuous distributions," the meaning of the numbers tends to become all but incomprehensible to those with little or no training in statistics. When confronted with complex statistics, the average person can do little more than seek out expert assistance, either in person on online. Along the same lines, it is important to understand how easy it is for an untrained person to completely misinterpret a complex statistic and spread that misinterpretation through advocacy. If, in looking at the primary source of a complex statistic, you cannot make heads or tails of the terminology and convoluted statistical formulas, what are the chances that an issue advocate with no training in statistics is going to understand and correctly interpret that primary source? In the hands of advocates, complex statistics can too often lead to wholesale misinterpretation.

Interpretation of Statistics

Over the last thirty or so years, the United States has seen crime rates drop. This phenomenon is so widely accepted as fact that it is safe to consider it common knowledge. What is left to interpretation, however, is *why* crime rates have declined. One person might look at the numbers and assert that crime dropped due to more police and tougher sentencing. Another might assert that the drop is due to such causes as an aging population and the success of antiviolence programs. Both of these interpretations of the drop in crime are (possibly) examples of what is called *hasty generalization* or *overgeneralization*—reaching a conclusion without necessarily understanding all of the factors that could be influencing the phenomenon in question. Even when given plenty of time to study the statistics and thoughtfully consider all possible factors, people will still disagree about what the statistics really mean. So even though those with an agenda to push or an argument to win may claim statistical authority, may assert that "the hard numbers prove I'm right," too often the numbers are not as hard as advertised and what they prove or disprove is less than clear-cut.

Another troubling aspect of the interpretation of statistics is when some-one misinterprets a statistic and that misinterpretation gets picked up and repeated by others. This is why going to the primary source to examine a statistic, versus accepting a statistic secondhand from someone who may have unintentionally (or intentionally) misinterpreted it, is key to evaluating the credibility of a statistic.

A FEW BASIC STATISTICAL CONCEPTS

The problem of complex statistics aside, it does not hurt to have an understanding of at least a few fundamental statistical concepts.

Percentage

Percentage is a ratio with a denominator of 100. If five out of twenty students are getting an A in a chemistry class, the ratio can be expressed as 5/20. The percentage of students getting an A can be calculated by finding the equivalent ratio whose denominator is 100. (The word *percentage* literally means "per 100.")

$$\frac{5}{20} = \frac{5 \times 5}{20 \times 5} = \frac{25}{100} = 25 \text{ percent}$$

Percentage has many uses, one of the most common being making comparisons among groups: "According to a recent poll, Proposition R is supported by 21 percent of voters who identify as Democrats, 47 percent of voters who identify as Independents, and 67 percent of voters who identify as Republicans." A common error is to confuse percentages with raw numbers. In the previous example, the 47 percent support among Independents most likely translates to many fewer voters than is represented by 21 percent of Democrats due to the fact that there are so many more Democrats than Independents. Another example of confusing percentage with raw numbers is seen in the example of course grades. In a chemistry class in which it is possible to earn a maximum of two thousand points during the course of the semester, missing a final grade of A by 2 percent is not the same as missing an A by two points. (With two thousand possible points, 2 percent is equal to forty points.)

Average

The tricky thing about the word *average* is that it can be used to describe a number of different mathematical concepts. The three types of averages you are likely to encounter are as follows.

Arithmetic Mean

Arithmetic mean is the sum of a collection of numbers divided by the number of numbers in that collection. Consider this example of annual incomes in table 6.2.

The arithmetic mean of the three annual salaries is $44,334.

$136,000 ÷ 3 = $44,334

Arithmetic mean is the most common way to determine average. One way that arithmetic mean can be misleading is when there is a skewed distribution. A skewed distribution occurs when one or a few numbers in a collection of numbers differ widely from other numbers in the collection. For example, if in the previous example the $57,000 annual salary were, instead, $570,000, the average of the three salaries would be $216,334, a figure that is not at all representative of the typical employee's salary.

Mode

Mode is the number that occurs most frequently in a collection of numbers. In the following collection of numbers representing grade point averages, the mode is 3.4.

1.7, 1.8, 2.9, 3.3, 3.4, 3.4, 3.4, 3.4, 3.7, 3.8, 4.0, 4.0

Mode is useful for understanding a skewed distribution when there are a few numbers on one or both extremes of a distribution. Mode can also be

Table 6.2. Example of Annual Incomes

Worker	Annual Income
Worker A	$57,000
Worker B	$37,000
Worker C	$42,000
Total	$136,000

used for nonnumerical data. For example, because white is the most popular color for automobiles, white can be considered the mode of car colors.

Median

Median represents the midpoint of any collection of numbers. Like mode, median is useful when an extreme outlier or two would otherwise skew an average. Say that in a rural community seventeen houses are for sale, with sixteen of those houses selling for between $120,00 and $250,000. However, the seventeenth house on the market happens to be the spectacular $15,500,000 mansion belonging to the hometown girl who made it big as a country music star. In such as case, the median price of houses for sale would give a much more realistic picture of what a prospective buyer might pay than would the average price.

No matter what the range of a collection of numbers may be, half of those numbers will be above the median while half will be below the median. This holds true regardless of how high or low those numbers may be. For example, if you ranked NFL Hall of Fame quarterbacks by career passer ratings, half of those Hall of Fame players would, by definition, fall below the median. Of course, this does not mean those players were bad quarterbacks; it merely means that they fell into the lower half of an extremely elite group. Indeed, a handful of completed passes over the course of a long career might be all that separates the lowest-ranked quarterback above the median from the highest-ranked quarterback below the median. By the same token, being above the median in a not-very-illustrious group—say, for example, the one hundred least-productive quarterbacks in NFL history—is not much of an achievement.

Margin of Error

When a random sample is used, the margin of error describes the amount of possible error due to the uncertainties of using a random sample. The smaller the margin of error, the more confidence there is that the random sample accurately represents the entire population.

Reliability and Validity

Reliability refers to the consistency of any measurement. For example, if a person were administered a psychological personality test three times and the results were consistent each time, the test would have high reliability.

Validity refers to how accurately something has been measured. If a preelection poll accurately predicts the outcome of the election, it has high validity.

One way to think of these two concepts is to use the metaphor of archery. If an archer were to shoot five arrows and they landed in a tight cluster, this represents a high degree of reliability (even if the group of arrows happened to be clustered far from the intended target). If the same archer were to shoot an arrow at a target and hit the center of the bulls-eye, this represents a high degree of validity. While every researcher strives for is both validity and reliability, the two concepts are separate phenomena and not intrinsically connected.

Statistical Significance

The phrase *statistically significant* sounds an awful lot like "The results of this study are true." But that is not what statistical significance actually means. Instead, what it means is that, by the standards of the study, the results are statistically significant. If the study itself is flawed—maybe the sample was not representative or errors were made during a laboratory experiment—the result of the study are still invalid even if the numbers came out as being statistically significant.

This previous lightning review of statistical concepts hardly scratches the surface of what there is to know about statistics. As mentioned before, anyone who really wants to become statistically literate needs to put some time and effort into studying the vast, complex, and fascinating subject of statistics.

RECAP

For all the ways in which statistics can mislead and/or be misused, they are too essential for understanding the human and natural worlds to be dismissed as mere hokum. Without statistics, human beings have no way of knowing how big or small a problem is or whether solutions to problems are actually working as intended. Or if solutions are working at all.

Evaluating statistics involves many of the same steps taken when evaluating any other form of information (see chapter 5). When presented with statistics, it is important to be aware that advocates often employ statistics in ways that can be misleading. For statistics to be credible, there must be clear definitions of what is being measured, samples must be truly representative, and comparisons cannot be apples to oranges. Statistical projections should be approached with caution, with the level of caution increasing the further into the future the projections extend. Surveys are powerful tools for assessing public opinion or quantifying human experiences, but the keys for survey credibility are (1) the representativeness of the sample and (2) the nature of the questions asked. Because statistics received secondhand may have been misinterpreted or misrepresented, thoroughly evaluating statistics requires examining the primary source that generated the statistics in the first place. And, finally, in spite of the fact that the numerical basis of statistics may make them seem inherently factual, the ultimate meaning of any statistic is open to greater or lesser levels of interpretation.

7

Scholarly Information

Identifying, Evaluating, and Understanding It

Scholarly information is a type of information created by people known as (surprise!) *scholars*. While anyone who attends school can be called a *scholar*, in the scholarly information sense of the word *scholar* refers to someone who is very learned in a particular field, usually as a result of advanced education and years of study. Scholars can be divided into two broad categories: academic scholars and nonacademic scholars.

Academic scholars include the faculty, other academic employees (postdoctoral researchers, lecturers, librarians, etc.), and (in some cases) students affiliated with institutions of higher education, chiefly universities and colleges. Academic scholars tend to be especially prolific when it comes to creating information because most of them are, to greater or lesser extents, evaluated on and rewarded for producing articles, books, data sets, and other scholarly information related to their research. *Nonacademic scholars* are those scholars not employed by, or otherwise directly affiliated with, institutions of higher education. Nonacademic scholars may work in government or private industry, though some nonacademic scholars work independently.

So why does scholarly information matter? It matters because scholarly information is how scholars share the results of their work, and the work of scholars is vitally important to the modern world. A study presented in 2017 found that academic scholars contributed to 74 percent of the most significant inventions created since 1950 and were "the most important or a very important actor in four in 10 cases."[1] (Note that these numbers do not include the substantial contributions of nonacademic scholars.) Whether the modern innovation is in health care, military technology, energy, or agriculture, scholars are likely part of that innovation's DNA. Arguably the most significant innovation of the last half century, the Internet, began as a university research project and remained as such for years before it was put to other uses. (Ironically, if not for academic scholars, online pundits and commentators would not have any platform on which to post their observations about everything that is wrong with higher education and why the world would be better off without it.)

Table 7.1 lists most of the major fields of scholarly studies arranged under four broad categories of scholarship. Note that some areas of study (such as history, law, and politics) fall under more than one category.

Innovations in science and technology are not the only way that scholars and scholarly information shape the world. In the arena of business, scholars often originate, test, and improve upon ideas impacting management, finance, and economic policy. Scholars in the arts, humanities, and social sciences contribute to the richness and greater understanding of the world's cultures. For example, independent scholar Ron Chernow's scholarly biography of Alexander Hamilton inspired the creation of the hit Broadway production *Hamilton! An American Musical*. Chernow does not work for a college or uni-

Table 7.1. Major Fields of Scholarly Studies under Four Broad Categories of Scholarship

Arts and Humanities	Social Sciences	Sciences	Technology
Anthropology	Anthropology	Agriculture	Aerospace engineering
Archaeology	Communications	Astronomy	Bioengineering
Classics	Economics	Biology	Civil engineering
History	Education	Chemistry	Computer engineering
Linguistics and languages	Geography	Computer Science	Electrical engineering
Law and Politics	History	Earth sciences	Information science
Literature	Law	Materials science	Mechanical engineering
Performing arts	Linguistics	Mathematics	Nanotechnology
Philosophy	Political science	Medicine	Nuclear engineering
Religion	Psychology	Physics	Robotics
Visual arts	Sociology	Statistics	Software engineering

Note: Some areas of study (such as history, law, and politics) fall under more than one category.

versity but, like most independent, nonacademic scholars, holds an academic degree and conducts research.

In addition to its impact on almost every facet of daily life, scholarly information is special because it represents the gold standard for information credibility. At least in the ideal to which honest scholars aspire, scholarly information is the most thoroughly researched, well-reasoned, well-vetted, and overall credible type of information humans can aspire to create. The goal of this chapter is to explain not only how to identify scholarly information, but also how scholarly information is created, the high standards to which it aspires, and why, in some cases, scholarly information fails to achieve its own high standards.

RESEARCH, SCHOLARS, AND SCHOLARLY INFORMATION

Around the world, a great deal of research is conducted at research universities. The faculty at research universities are expected to conduct original research and publish the results of that research. Research universities also employ nonfaculty academics who conduct research, including many postdoctoral researchers (commonly known as *postdocs*). A postdoc is an academic researcher who has completed a doctorate but is employed as academic staff rather than as faculty (i.e., postdocs are not professors). Finally, research universities are home to large cohorts of graduate students, most of whom conduct research under the guidance of one or more faculty members while pursuing an advanced degree. Non-research universities, four-year colleges, and two-year colleges tend to emphasize teaching over research; however, the faculty of such institutions may conduct research and create scholarly information in addition to teaching.

When academic scholars conduct research, they typically publish the results of that research in order to share it widely. Especially in the STEM fields (science, technology, engineering, and mathematics) the most important type of publication is the scholarly article. In the arts and humanities, the book remains the most important form of publication. In the social sciences, there is a split between the importance of books and articles, with some social science fields emphasizing articles, some fields emphasizing books, and some treating both forms as equally important. Which is not to say that there is no crossover: physicists publish books just as surely as historians publish scholarly articles. In addition, scholars in all fields are increasingly publishing in new formats made possible by digital technology. For example, in the last decade a new field of study known as "digital humanities" has emerged in which digital technologies are applied to the study of such traditional humanities fields as history, literature, anthropology, and philosophy.

Faculty stand to reap personal rewards for the information they create when they go up for promotion or tenure, a formal review process that typically involves a committee of senior faculty reviewing a junior faculty member's professional portfolio. While promotion-and-tenure committees consider a faculty member's entire professional portfolio (teaching, publications, research, grants received, and service), the quantity and quality of scholarly information a faculty member has published often weighs heavily on whether promotion or tenure are awarded. The importance of publication in the promotion-and-tenure process is the inspiration for the saying "publish or perish." Nonfaculty researchers—such as postdocs and nonacademic scholars working in government or private industry—also publish the results of their research but are not typically subject to formal promotion-and-tenure processes.

Graduate students may also publish articles and (less commonly) books prior to graduation. Having published while still a student enhances a graduate student's prospects of landing a desirable job postgraduation. The most important publication for a graduate student is either the thesis or the dissertation. A typical thesis is a major research paper and the final requirement for earning a master's degree. A dissertation is required to complete most doctoral degree programs. Written under the guidance of a faculty adviser, the thesis or dissertation is the graduate student's magnum opus (literally, "great work"). The classic doctoral dissertation is a book-length work focused on a fairly narrow academic topic, based on original research, and organized as follows:

- Introduction: background, thesis statement, and literature review
- Middle chapters: methods, results, discussion
- Final chapter: conclusion

There are exceptions to the classic dissertation format. In some fields, it is possible for a graduate student to produce what is known as a *thesis by publication* in place of a traditional dissertation. Rather than being a coherent, book-like composition, a thesis by publication is a collection of the graduate student's previously published articles, book chapters, and/or conference papers. In the fine arts fields, a thesis may take the form of a creative work, such as a novel, screenplay, musical composition, portfolio of artworks, or film. Writers of traditional theses and dissertations formally cite sources in accordance with the style guide that applies to their area of study. Following graduation, authors may seek to have their thesis or dissertation published in book form by an academic or commercial press, a process that usually involves considerable revision.

Scholars employed by private industry often work in research and development. While these nonacademic scholars may publish the results of their research, they are rewarded more for their contribution to the company's bottom line than for their contributions to scholarship. In cases where a nonacademic scholar's research may lead to patentable ideas, the scholar may be prohibited from publishing in order to protect the company's financial interests.

Federal, state, and local government agencies also employ scholars who conduct research. For example, the US Department of Agriculture employs plant scientists to do research related to agricultural productivity, while the US Department of Energy runs huge research laboratories employing thousands of research scientists studying topics ranging from nanoparticles to computational science. Government scientists are generally allowed and encouraged to publish the results of their research except where national security concerns take precedence.

Scholars publish scholarly information both to share what they know with the world and to reap the rewards that come with publication. In addition to the role publications play in promotion and tenure, publications also help establish scholars' status among their professional peers. If there were such a thing as baseball cards for scholars, the back sides of those cards would list the scholars' publications.

THE SCIENTIFIC METHOD

A model for studying both the natural and human worlds, the *scientific method* is employed by scientists, technologists, and social scientists around the world. In fact, you probably use a simplified form of the scientific method in your daily life without really realizing it:

You wake up in the morning to the sound of water drops hitting your window. This provokes a question: "Is it raining?"

This question then provokes a hypothesis: "I believe it is raining."

You test your hypothesis by opening the curtains to look outside. Water droplets are falling from low, gray clouds. The ground is wet. Water drips from trees and bushes. People walking by hold umbrellas over their heads. You have made an observation and collected information.

You analyze what you have observed and come to a conclusion: "My hypothesis is confirmed by the empirical evidence. It is raining."

As a rational person, in reaching your conclusion you eliminate unlikely possibilities not supported by the empirical evidence you observed while looking out the window:

- "It is unlikely that the fire department is pranking me by spraying water from a fire truck parked just out of sight."

- "Because I live over two hundred miles from the coast, it is unlikely that the drops are coming from the blowhole of an exceptionally large whale."

(Common sense, it turns out, plays an important role in the scientific method.)

Finally, you announce, "Hey, it's raining," as a way of sharing your knowledge.

The scientific method is, in its fullest form, a complex and nuanced concept. In addition, the specific ways in which the scientific method is applied vary from discipline to discipline and from researcher to researcher. That said, the basic idea of the scientific method is rather straightforward: the acquisition of new knowledge must follow a rational process that commonly involves formulating a hypothesis, testing the hypothesis through the observation of empirical evidence, analyzing the evidence, and reaching a conclusion.

Another important tenet of the scientific method is that results must be reproducible. Suppose a pair of educational researchers develop and test a new method of teaching mathematics to elementary students. The researchers eventually publish a scholarly article that concludes that their new teaching method results in students achieving significantly higher scores on standardized math tests. However, when other educational researchers repeat the experiment by employing the new teaching method with students, their results show no improvement in test scores. As long as other researchers are unable to reproduce the original researchers' results, the conclusion that the new teaching method is superior cannot be considered valid under the rules of the scientific method. On the other hand, if a chemist observes that heat of vaporization for mercury is 59.11 kJ/mol and other chemists independently confirm that this observation is accurate, the observation must be considered scientifically valid unless and until new empirical evidence proves otherwise.

One way to envision the scientific method is think of it as a cycle of questioning, testing, observation, and analysis in which every new study builds on the results of previous studies (see figure 7.1).

Research studies that employ the scientific method's principles of forming a hypothesis, testing the hypothesis, and observing the results are known as *empirical studies*. Empirical studies that produce numerical data are known as *quantitative research*. Research that is more exploratory in approach is known as *qualitative research*. Qualitative research is conducted in order to gain a broad understanding of what is being studied. Common methods of qualitative research include focus groups, surveys, and interviews, often involving small sample sizes that are not intended to be representative of entire populations. For example, psychologists in London conducted a qualitative study "to understand the experience over time of home-dwelling older people deemed frail, in order to enhance the evidence base for person-centred [sic] approaches to frail elder care."[2] The researchers employed a combination of sophisticated qualitative research techniques that involved visiting and observing the subjects of the study. As happens with qualitative studies, the

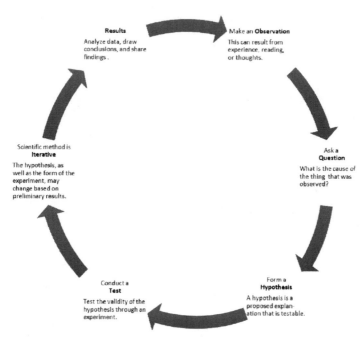

FIGURE 7.1
The cycle of the scientific method. *Donald A. Barclay*

preceding qualitative study on home-dwelling frail elders was later used to inform a follow-up quantitative study of frail elderly persons.[3]

Scholarly information plays in important role in the scientific method. First of all, reading scholarly information leads researchers to make observations and ask questions. Say, for example, while reading a scholarly article about the role of race in voter turnout, a political scientist formulates a research question. This research question leads, in turn, to a new testable hypothesis about race and voter turnout. Next, the political scientist searches the scholarly literature for examples of applicable methods for testing the new hypothesis, eventually finding a survey and adapting it for the purpose of researching voter turnout (see figure 7.2). After completing the research, the political scientist creates new scholarly information in the form of a scholarly journal article and a related data set.

One important point about the scientific method is that it is more of a philosophy about how humans gain knowledge than a one-size-fits-all formula.

FIGURE 7.2
A researcher in the field collects data that will later be analyzed to test the researcher's hypothesis. *Elena Zhukova, University of California, Merced*

A second important point is that the scientific method does not bestow infallibility on researchers or the results they produce. As mere human beings, researchers who employ the scientific method may intentionally cheat, make mistakes, or interpret the same findings in different ways. Even so, the scientific method is the best method available for creating credible information.

IDENTIFYING THE FORMATS OF SCHOLARLY INFORMATION

If scholarly information is so special, a good question to ask is "How do I know if information is scholarly or not?" One way to identify scholarly information is to become familiar with the most common formats in which it appears.

Scholarly Journals

Teachers and professors often instruct students to use articles from scholarly journals in their research, though they may not use the exact words "scholarly journals." Synonyms for scholarly journal include

- academic journal
- professional journal

- peer-reviewed journal
- refereed journal

To avoid confusion, this book will use the term *scholarly journal* to signify all of the above. The purpose of the scholarly journal is to allow scholars to share information—primarily information reporting original research—with other scholars. The first scholarly journals started appearing in the middle of the seventeenth century, a product of the Age of Enlightenment and the scientific revolution that was at the time taking hold throughout Europe. A study published in 2009 found there were 26,406 active scholarly journals.[4] (The exact numbers are not easy to pin down.) During the first decade of the twenty-first century, almost all scholarly journals transitioned from print to online publication, with online publication now being the dominant format though which scholarly journals are distributed and accessed. The best way to know if you are looking at a scholarly journal is to become familiar with the characteristics that identify a publication as a scholarly journal.

One characteristic of scholarly journals is that most have a specific subject focus. The following scholarly journals, each of which focuses on a relatively narrow subject area, are typical:

- *Journal of Modern Literature*
- *Chaucer Review*
- *Research in African Literature*
- *Western American Literature*
- *Eighteenth-Century Fiction*

The preceding list consists of just five of the hundreds of scholarly literature journals published around the world, most of which focus on a distinct field of literary studies. There are exceptions to the rule that scholarly journals have a specific subject focus—one example is the well-regarded scholarly journal *Science*, which publishes articles on a variety of scientific topics—but such exceptions are few.

The true hallmark of scholarly journals is that they feature scholarly articles (described in detail later) written by scholars rather than nonscholarly articles written by journalists. For example, in August of 2017 a team of physicists published in the scholarly journal *Science* an article about an experiment in which they successfully desalinated water using carbon nanotubes.[5] The target audience for their article was other scientists and engineers with research interests in desalination and/or nanotubes. Because the potential practical applications of the physicists' work made for a newsworthy story, journalists quickly wrote *popular* news stories about the physicists' findings. One such example is a story published in the Verge, a news and media network that reports on technology for an audience of general readers.[6] Even though both articles are reporting the same event, the article written by physicists and published in the journal *Science* is scholarly while the article written by a journalist and published in the Verge is popular rather than scholarly.

Not every item published in a scholarly journal is necessarily a scholarly article. In addition to scholarly articles, scholarly journals may also publish

- letters commenting on previously published articles
- editorials expressing opinions on topics relating to the journal's subject focus
- news stories relating to the journal's subject focus
- errata correcting errors contained in previously published articles
- reviews of books relating to the journal's subject focus
- announcements of upcoming conferences

Unlike popular magazines, most scholarly journals do not carry advertisements, though there are exceptions. Advertisements for relevant scholarly books are published in many scholarly journals, while advertisements for medications and medical equipment appear in a number of medical journals.

Scholarly journals are overseen by editorial boards: teams of volunteer scholars who set editorial standards and provide high-level guidance on the management and long-term goals of the journal. The more prestigious a journal, the more prestigious the membership of its editorial board.

Peer Review

Most, though not all, scholarly journals employ peer review. In a publication that does not employ peer review—such as a magazine, newspaper, or web-based publication aimed at a popular audience—an author submits an article to an editor who ultimately decides (possibly in consultation with other editors) whether to accept the article for publication. It is also up to the editor (or editors) to call for any changes necessary to render the article suitable for publication. In contrast, in a peer-reviewed journal the author submits an article to an editor, who makes an initial decision about whether the article might be right for the journal. The editor then sends out a copy of the article to a group of two or more *referees*, who read the article, decide if it should be accepted for publication, and suggest any changes. In the world of scholarly journals, referees are scholars with expertise in the topic addressed by the article. For example, an article on radiation oncology would be sent to referees who are experts in radiation oncology. An article on congressional redistricting would be sent to referees who are experts on congressional redistricting. And so on. The most rigorous form of peer review is *blind peer review*, in which the name of the author is removed from the copies sent to the referees so that their decisions are not influenced by what they may previously know, or not know, about the author. The referees send their recommendations and comments back to the editor, who then communicates with the author. If scholarly publication is the gold standard for credible information, then peer review is the gold standard for scholarly publication. Properly carried out, peer review ensures that all published articles meet a high standard of scholarship and that they are impartially evaluated on their scholarly merit.

How do you know if a journal employs peer review? On a peer-reviewed journal's website, there will usually be information about its peer-review process in either the "About" section or the "Information for Authors" section. Most scholarly journals have an entry in *Wikipedia* that will tell you if the journal is peer reviewed, though the usual cautions about using *Wikipedia* apply (see chapter 5). If your library provides access to the online publication *UlrichsWEB*, you can look up a journal by title and find information about whether or not it employs peer review. (Note that some journals will use the word *refereed* in place of, or interchangeably with, *peer review*.)

Journal Rankings

In most fields of scholarship there is a definite pecking order for scholarly journals in which they are ranked according to prestige. The traditional way to rank journals is by *impact factor*. The basic idea of the impact factor is that the more often articles published in *Journal X* are cited by other scholars, the higher *Journal X*'s impact factor. As a rule, scholars strive to publish in highly ranked journals on the grounds that doing so enhances a scholar's professional reputation.

In recent years the concept of impact factor has become controversial, especially when it is used as a means of evaluating individual scholars, something that was never the intended purpose of the impact factor.[7] Scholars are increasingly considering a variety of evaluation tools collectively known as *altmetrics* as an alternative or supplement to impact factors.[8] Even so, scholars—especially academic scholars in the STEM fields—continue to feel pressure to publish in highly ranked journals as a mark of professional prestige.

PREDATORY JOURNALS

At the bottom of the journal rankings lie predatory journals, a type of online publication that looks a lot like a scholarly journal but does not behave like one. A phenomenon of the Digital Age, predatory journals actively (some would say *aggressively*) solicit papers from scholarly authors. Predatory journals require that authors pay a fee known as an *article publication charge* (APC) before a paper is published, often failing to mention the fee until after the scholar's paper has been accepted. But here is the catch: unlike legitimate scholarly journals, predatory journals accept just about every paper that is submitted. While predatory journals claim to employ peer review and enforce rigorous editorial standards, they do neither, publishing papers based on an author's willingness to pay an APC and without any regard for the quality of the research or the writing. Predatory journals also often lie about their rankings and impact factors in order to convince scholars to buy into the predatory journals' pay-to-publish scheme. In short, predatory journals are moneymaking scams whose editors will publish just about anything for a price. Some scholars who publish in predatory journals do so unwittingly, though an unscrupulous scholar will turn to predatory journals as an easy means of padding the list of publications in his or her curriculum vitae (the scholar's version of a résumé). This strategy fails, however, if professional colleagues discover that the articles listed in a scholar's curriculum vitae were actually published in predatory journals.

Telling the difference between a predatory journal and a legitimate scholarly journal can be difficult. First of all, the fact that a journal charges an APC *does not* mean that it is a predatory journal. Many legitimate scholarly journals accept APCs. The reason authors pay APCs to legitimate journals is so that their articles can be immediately published in open access formats that are free for anyone to read. (See the later description of open access publishing.) The difference between legitimate scholarly journals and predatory journals is that legitimate scholarly journals hold every submitted article to a high standard of peer review and/or editorial rigor. Unlike predatory journals, legitimate scholarly journals do not accept and publish substandard articles in order to pocket APCs.

For several years an academic librarian named Jeffrey Beall singlehandedly maintained a blog called *Beall's List of Predatory Journals and Publishers*; however, Beall gave up maintaining his blog in January 2017.[9] Shortly after Jeffery Beall stopped maintaining *Beall's List* came the launch of the *Journal Blacklist*, an online, subscription-based publication that lists and evaluates predatory journals.[10]

If your library doesn't have a subscription to the *Journal Blacklist*, the Directory of Open Access Journals (https://doaj.org), which has recently strengthened its criteria for inclusion to weed out predatory journals, is a useful open access tool for evaluating journals. Think. Check. Submit (http://thinkchecksubmit.org) is yet another useful open access resource. Intended to help authors identify predatory journals before they submit manuscripts, Think. Check. Submit is also useful for separating the legitimate journals from the predators. In addition to consulting these resources, a good first step in determining a journal's credibility is to visit its website:

- If the journal's website does not look very professional, the journal may be predatory. Try comparing the website of a suspect journal with the website of a scholarly journal that is known to be legitimate. In most cases, the difference will be striking.

- Look at the information the journal provides for prospective authors. If the journal emphasizes quick peer review or otherwise promises quick turnaround times between submission and publication, it may be a predatory journal.

- Run a few of the names listed as members of the journal's editorial board through a search engine to see if they are qualified scholars. Be aware that predatory journals are known to list as editors people with no real scholarly qualifications.[11]

- Journals that accept papers from broad areas of knowledge rather than focusing on a specific subfield may be predatory journals, though there are exceptions (such as the scholarly journal *Science* mentioned earlier).

- If a journal charges APCs, then the terms of the APCs, including cost, should be easy to find on the journal's website. Predatory journals often keep the cost of APC hidden until after the author's work has been accepted.

- If a journal claims to be endorsed by an outside organization, visit that organization's website and/or run the organization's name through a search engine to see if it is legitimate. (Be aware that predatory journals may falsely claim to be endorsed by organizations to which they have no real connection.)

- If you can determine that a journal has been publishing for many decades, this is a sign that it is *not* a predatory journal. While there certainly are legitimate journals that have been publishing for only a few years, no predatory journals have been publishing for thirty, forty, fifty, or more years. In fact, it is highly unlikely that any journal that was publishing articles prior to the year 2000 would turn out to be a predatory journal.

- While you certainly cannot trust every random comment you read online, if a search of the title of a suspect journal along with the phrase "predatory journal" turns up multiple instances of what seem to be legitimate scholars labeling the journal as predatory, that is not a good sign for the journal's legitimacy.

Though none of these markers is, by itself, smoking-gun evidence that a journal is predatory, if several of the markers apply, then there is a good chance the journal is predatory. Business ethics aside, the real problem with predatory journals is that they undermine the credibility of scholarship by dressing up noncredible information in the clothing of the scholarly article—perhaps the most credible form of information there is. While it is hard to be fooled by a raving blog post written by someone who clearly has no idea what they are talking about, it is much easier to be fooled by a piece of writing that looks and reads exactly like a scholarly article and is published in a predatory journal doing its best to pass itself off as a legitimate scholarly journal.

Scholarly Articles

Scholarly articles are the bedrock of scholarly journals. The most common type of scholarly article reports original research, such as an experiment, a study, or other new discovery. It is possible for a scholarly article to have more than one author; indeed, in many STEM fields multiple coauthors are more common than single authors. Although not every scholarly article contains all of the following features, these features are typically part of the format of scholarly articles in the STEM fields and the social sciences:

- *Abstract*: a one-paragraph summary of the article.
- *Introduction*: background information that provides context for the research, such as why the research was done in the first place or a statement of the problem under consideration. The introduction will also include a

thesis statement (a sentence that summarizes the main point or claim of the article) or a hypothesis (a statement that can be proved or disproved).

- *Literature review*: a list and discussion of previously published studies on the topic covered by the article.
- *Methods*: a description of how the research was conducted. This could include such things as the procedures followed during an experiment, the sampling techniques used, the survey questions asked, and so on. The methods section should describe the research in enough detail that another researcher could replicate the research in order to either verify or disprove its findings.
- *Results*: a summary description of the findings of the research. Results can be numerical, as when the results section of a study on airline travel delays finds that 8 percent of delays experienced by budget air carriers are due to weather conditions. On the other hand, results can be nonnumerical, as when a qualitative study of job satisfaction among a focus group of elementary school teachers finds that burnout does not seem to be a concern among teachers with less than ten years in the classroom.
- *Discussion*: a section that addresses the limitations of the study, compares the study to other studies, and describes possible areas for future research.
- *Conclusion*: the final summing-up of the article.
- *Works cited*: a list of all the works formally cited in the article. The "Works Cited" section may go by a number of other names, including "References," "Notes," or "Bibliography."
- *Appendixes*: sections that might include such items as survey questions, charts, illustrations, and so on.
- A *DOI* (digital object identifier): a number used to permanently identify a digital object such as an article, data set, or report. Unlike a URL, which can vanish or change, a DOI stays with its assigned object regardless of where that object may be found on the Internet. While DOIs may be applied to objects other than scholarly journal articles, almost every online scholarly journal article has a unique DOI. Citations found in scholarly databases (such as Google Scholar and the subject-focused scholarly databases listed in table 7.2) usually include DOIs for scholarly articles. Also, a DOI usually appears on the first page of a scholarly article. Example of a DOI: dx.doi.org/10.1080/01616846.2017.1327767.

In fields outside of STEM and the social sciences, scholarly articles may take forms that vary from what is described here. For example, in journals devoted to literary criticism, articles tend to take the form of nuanced essays that interpret one or more literary works. As a rule, articles in arts and humanities journals are more free form than those found in STEM and social science journals.

Review Articles

Another important type of article published in scholarly journals is the *review article*. Rather than reporting on original research, a review article broadly considers all the previous published research on a specific, typically quite narrow topic. After introducing the topic to be covered, a review article will list and evaluate significant publications on that topic. A review article may also identify the leading individuals doing research in the field, the major foci of current research, gaps in the research, and possible future directions for research. Because of their broad approach, review articles can be especially helpful for introducing a nonexpert to an unfamiliar area of study.

A special type of review article is the *systematic review*. The authors of a systematic review consider the published research on a particular topic and, through sophisticated statistical analysis, summarize the consensus of all that research. Systematic reviews are especially useful in medicine, where they can be used to point out the scientific consensus of multiple clinical trials. For example, if there have been ten separate clinical trials testing the safety and effectiveness of drug X for treating lower back pain, a systematic review will bring together the results of those ten clinical trials, synthesize their collective findings, and point to the current *scientific consensus*. Scientific consensus is an important concept in that it reflects the collective (though not unanimous) thinking of the community of scientists in a specific field of study. Even though scientific consensus can change as new evidence emerges, the scientific consensus on any topic tends to be right far more often than it is wrong. Review articles typically have the word *review* in the title, and the advanced search feature of some subject-focused databases allow searchers to limit search results to review articles only.

The following is an actual example of the power of a systematic review. In the early 1970s many claims were being made about the medicinal value of vitamin C (ascorbic acid). One of the people making such claims was the distinguished chemist and biochemist Linus Pauling. One of the most influential and important scientists of the twentieth century, Pauling was the recipient of two Nobel Prizes—one for chemistry (in 1954) and one for peace (in 1962). As you might imagine, when a scientist with the well-deserved credibility of Linus Pauling talks about the virtues of vitamin C, people listen. But not everyone was convinced. In 1975 a researcher analyzed the results of fourteen clinical trials testing the ability of vitamin C to prevent and treat the common cold. In his published systematic review the researcher concluded that "the very minor potential benefit that might result from taking ascorbic acid three times a day for life" was not "worth either the effort or the risk, no matter how slight the latter might be."[12] Additional original research resulted in the scientific consensus that taking vitamin C does little or nothing for those suffering from the common cold. Besides demonstrating the power and usefulness of systematic reviews, this example illustrates another point about scholarly information—no matter how great an individual's contributions to knowledge and scholarly reputation may be, no scholar's word is law and every scholar's hypotheses must meet the same standards of proof required of every other scholar.

Conference Proceedings

Conference proceedings, which are sometimes known as simply *proceedings*, are published collections of papers presented at scholarly conferences. Similar in format to scholarly articles, papers presented at conferences may end up being revised and published as scholarly articles. In some cases, the papers that make up the proceedings of a conference may be collectively published as a special issue of, or supplement to, a scholarly journal. The rigor of acceptance standards for conference papers varies from one conference to the next. For some conferences, papers are accepted or rejected based on the decision of a single reviewer, while other conferences employ peer review and require revision before a paper is accepted for presentation. Because a conference paper can be shared on a shorter time line than is required for a published article, conference papers are important for sharing cutting-edge research, especially in fast-moving STEM fields. Presenting a paper at an important conference may, in some cases, be as prestigious as publishing an article in a scholarly journal.

Conference proceedings can usually be identified by virtue of having the name of a conference somewhere in the title. For example:

- *International Conference on AC and DC Power Transmission*
- *Proceedings of the Second International Workshop on Object Orientation in Operating Systems*
- *IEE Colloquium on RACE Optical Systems and Demonstrators*

Scholarly Monographs

A scholarly monograph is a book written by a scholar and focused on a single topic. For example, Brian M. Ingrassia's *The Rise of Gridiron University: Higher Education's Uneasy Alliance with Big-Time Football* is a scholarly monograph on the early history of college football. Stephen J. Gould's *The Structure of Evolutionary Theory* is a scholarly monograph on the topic of evolutionary theory. Henry Petroski's *Design Paradigms: Case Histories of Error and Judgment in Engineering* is a scholarly monograph on the topic of engineering mistakes. As the three examples suggest, one characteristic of scholarly monographs is that their titles usually provide accurate descriptions of what the monograph is about. Another characteristic of scholarly monographs is that they are often, though not always, published by university presses or the presses of scholarly societies; with some exceptions, scholars hold publication via such presses to be more prestigious than publication via commercial presses. Like scholarly articles, scholarly monographs include formal citations in the form of footnotes, endnotes, and/or bibliographies.

A scholarly monograph can be part of a *monographic series*—a set of scholarly monographs in which each work stands on its own while all the works in the series are connected through a unifying theme. For example, the American Academy of Ophthalmology Monograph Series is a series of monographs on ophthalmological topics that is published by Oxford University Press.

Edited Scholarly Books

An edited scholarly book (often simply called an edited book) consists of a collection of chapters written by different scholars in which all the chapters are focused on a single unifying theme. Take, for example, the edited book *Sacred Darkness: A Global Perspective on the Ritual Use of Caves*. The editor of this book is Holley Moyes, an archaeology professor. As is common for an edited scholarly book, Moyes, as editor, wrote the introduction to the book. The bulk of the book consists of chapters written by various scholarly authors. While all of the chapters in *Sacred Darkness* relate to the central theme of the ritual use of caves, each chapter functions very much like a stand-alone scholarly article. Besides serving as editor, Moyes is the coauthor of two of the chapters included in *Sacred Darkness*. It is common for an editor of an edited scholarly book to author (or coauthor) one or more of the chapters included in the book.

Other Types of Scholarly Books

A *scholarly anthology* is a book that is composed of previously published works. These works might be journal articles, fiction, poetry, book chapters, selections from books, or primary source materials. The editor (or editors) of a scholarly anthology will typically write a substantial introduction to the entire anthology as well shorter introductions to sections of the anthology and/or individual works included in the anthology. One example of a scholarly anthology is *The Anthology of Rap*, edited by Adam Bradley, Andrew DuBois; Henry Louis Gates Jr., Chuck D, and Common. Published by Yale University Press in 2010, *The Anthology of Rap* is a collection of three hundred rap lyrics chosen to represent the wealth and diversity of rap music's poetic tradition.

A *textbook* is specifically written for students to use in a course. A textbook may cover either a broad subject area (e.g., *Introduction to Psychology*) or focus on a narrow topic (e.g., *Defect and Impurity-Engineered Semiconductors and Devices*). Textbooks may include features such as review questions, homework problems, and quizzes. The format of a textbook may be print, digital, or both. Besides its role as a course text, a well-written textbook can provide a good introduction to a subject.

Reference books (print or digital) contain information that is intended to be quickly looked up and read in small doses. Examples of reference works include encyclopedias, dictionaries, handbooks, almanacs, and catalogs. In the twenty-first century, digital publication has become the dominant format for reference works. The venerable *Encyclopaedia Britannica* stopped producing print copies in 2012 and has since existed as an online-only publication.[13] Reference works are considered scholarly if they employ high editorial standards and the contents are written by scholars. An example of a scholarly reference work is the freely available *Stanford Encyclopedia of Philosophy* (plato.stan ford.edu), which is comprised of contributions from scholars in philosophy and related fields.

Dissertations and Theses

As described earlier, dissertations and theses are written by graduate students in order to complete their degree programs. In addition to their subject content, theses and dissertations typically contain substantial bibliographies that are extremely useful for locating scholarly information relevant to the subject content.

Emerging Formats for Scholarly Information

Increasingly, scholarly research is shared via formats that do not fit into traditional forms of publication.[14] Databases, software, digital maps, videos, and other digital formats are taking their rightful place alongside traditional publications as part of the twenty-first-century scholar's professional portfolio. One such example, the family of scholarly journals published under the *JoVE* (*Journal of Visualized Experimentation*) trademark, consists entirely of peer-reviewed scholarly videos documenting scientific experiments. Another example is Valley of the Shadow: Two Communities in the American Civil War (valley.lib.virginia.edu). A digital humanities archive focusing on one northern and one southern community in the Civil War, Valley of the Shadow is a searchable archive that includes data on population, agriculture, manufacturing, and slavery as well as diaries, maps, images, and other primary-source materials.

DOLLARS AND SCHOLARS:
THE ECONOMICS OF SCHOLARLY INFORMATION

Because both research and publication come with price tags attached, it is no surprise that money plays a role in the production of scholarly information.

Writing for (Non) Profit

Unlike journalists, novelists, and other writers, scholars are typically not paid, or are paid very little, for their scholarly writing. In the case of scholarly articles, scholars receive no payment from the scholarly journals in which they publish. Why do scholars give away their articles for free? One reason is

USING SUBJECT-FOCUSED DATABASES TO FIND SCHOLARLY INFORMATION

There are several hundred subject-focused databases that provide information about, and often direct links to, scholarly articles, books, and other scholarly information resources. A few prominent examples of subject-focused databases are shown in table 7.2.

Table 7.2. Examples of Subject-Focused Scholarly Databases

Database	Subject Focus
America: History and Life	U.S. and Canadian history
Ei Compendex	Engineering
MLA International Bibliography	Modern languages and literature
PsycInfo	Behavioral and social science
SciFinder Scholar	Chemistry

The advantage of using a database that is both scholarly and subject focused rather than, say, a general-purpose search engine, is that most, if not all, of the information you retrieve with the former will be scholarly rather than a mix of scholarly and popular information. At the same time, the information will be relevant to the subject on which the database is focused. Many subject-focused databases offer advanced search features typically not found in general-purpose search engines, such as

- limiting search results to empirical studies
- limiting search results to review articles
- providing information on the number of times an article has been cited and by whom
- limiting search results to specific scholarly formats (articles, book chapters, dissertations, etc.)

Because most scholarly, subject-focused databases require a subscription, access will usually be through a subscription provided by a library. When you visit your library's home page, look for a link that says something like "Databases" or "Find Articles" in order to determine which databases are available.

Google Scholar (scholar.google.com) is a free search engine that is a powerful tool for finding scholarly information, mostly articles and books. Rather than being subject-focused, Google Scholar covers all areas of scholarly study. One especially useful (though not unique) feature provided by Google Scholar is direct links to open access versions of articles. (See later in the chapter for information on open access.)

that most scholars are more interested in sharing their findings with others than with profiting directly from their writing. Another reason is that scholars who publish journal articles stand to later reap rewards in the form of promotion and tenure earned, at least in part, through their scholarly publications. Similarly, scholars who serve as referees for, or sit on the editorial boards of, scholarly journals are not paid by the journals for their services. However, many academic scholars are expected to serve as referees or members of editorial boards as part of their job duties, and service on highly ranked journals contributes to a scholar's overall professional reputation and prestige.

In the case of scholarly books, authors are paid royalties based on the number of copies sold. For most scholarly books, author royalties do not add up to significant amounts of money, though the rare scholarly book sells well enough to produce significant royalties. A successful textbook, on the other hand, is likely to generate significant royalties for a scholarly author. As is the case with publishing journal articles, publishing a scholarly book is a pathway to promotion and tenure, especially for academic scholars in the arts and humanities.

Grant Funding

The most significant impact of money on scholarly information is in the funding of research through grants. Unsurprisingly, it costs money to conduct research. Depending on the field of study, research costs may include such expenses as travel, equipment, information technology, materials, support staff, publication costs, and so on. Some forms of research, such as traditional humanities research, are not particularly costly while other forms, such as major research projects involving advanced science and technology, can cost millions. In order to conduct research, scholars typically seek out grants, principally from government agencies but also from private funders. Because most grants are awarded on a competitive basis, there exists a grant/research/ publication cycle in which grants feed research, research feeds publication, and publication feeds grants. Just as a scholar's record of publication plays a role in promotion and tenure, it also plays a role in a scholar's ability to secure grants that, in turn, play a role in promotion and tenure.

Open Access Publishing

The business of publishing scholarly journals operates on an economic model that is perhaps unique. Original research is funded through grants (most of which are, in turn, funded by taxpayers). The articles resulting from grant-funded research are published by scholarly journals that don't pay authors, referees, or editorial board members for their services. When the articles are finally published, academic libraries pay for subscriptions to scholarly journals, often using tax dollars to do so.

Each year, the sums paid to the publishers of scholarly journals are not small. Worldwide, the scholarly information marketplace annually grosses about 10 billion dollars.[15] Publishers contend that the high cost of scholarly information is justified due to the large amount of work required to manage peer review, prepare manuscripts for publication, and publish the final versions of articles. While nobody denies that there are real costs associated with publishing scholarly articles, the fact that for-profit publishers of scholarly information have consistently returned some of the highest profit margins of any type of business is troubling to many scholars.[16] The annual cost of scholarly information—in particular, the cost of scholarly journal subscriptions in the STEM fields—consumes an ever-growing chunk of academic library budgets, leading many academic librarians and scholars to the conclusion that it is possible for scholars to reclaim ownership of their scholarly articles and, by making articles freely available via the Internet, greatly reduce the costs of scholarly publishing while simultaneously making articles freely available to all. This vision for scholarly publishing is known as *open access*.

For libraries, the attraction of open access publishing is that it could reduce the huge financial burden of academic journal subscriptions. For scholars, open access means that their work can be read by anyone, regardless of ability to pay. As a bonus, the fact that open access publications tend to get cited more than publications that are behind a paywall means that publishing open access increases a scholar's impact. (In the jargon of open access, the phrase *behind a paywall* refers to publications that require a subscription or other payment before they can be accessed.)

While there are many versions of open access, the two main forms are *gold open access* and *green open access*.

Gold Open Access

In the gold open access model, the author pays a one-time APC ensuring that, from the moment it is published, the article will be freely and permanently available to anyone with access to the Internet. The funds for paying APCs usually come from grants or institutional funds rather than out of the scholar's pocket. Gold open access scholarly journals may be for profit or nonprofit. *Hybrid journals* is the term for journals that publish both open access articles (for which the author has paid an APC) as well as articles that remain behind a paywall (the author has not paid an APC).

Green Open Access

In the green open access model, authors self-archive their articles by depositing copies into an open access repository. When an article is originally published in a scholarly journal, there may be an embargo period (usually one year) between the time the article first appears in the scholarly journal and when the author may legally deposit a version of the article in a green open access repository. In some cases a *preprint* (the author's final manuscript version of the article) is deposited rather than the final published version of the article as it appears in the journal.

Academic scholars often deposit articles in *institutional open access repositories* managed by the college or university for which they work. Examples of institutional open access repositories include the University of California's eScholarship (escholarship.org) and the University of Kansas's KU Scholar Works (kuscholarworks.ku.edu).

A second version of the open access repository is the *discipline-based repository* in which papers from related fields of study (a.k.a. *disciplines*) are deposited. A leading example of a discipline-based repository is the *arXiv* (arxiv .org) repository that brings together preprints of articles from the disciplines of physics, mathematics, computer science, quantitative biology, quantitative finance, and statistics.

Yet another type of green open access repository is represented by PubMed Central, a government open access repository managed by the US National Institutes of Health's National Library of Medicine. In August 2017, PubMed Central contained 4.4 million open access articles.[17] The reason for the large number of articles in PubMed Central is that, beginning in 2008, it became a requirement that all articles published as a result of grant funding provided by the National Institutes of Health be deposited in PubMed Central no later than twelve months after publication in a journal or other outlet. Around the world, an increasing number of grant funding entities, both governmental and private, have instituted similar policies requiring that articles originating from the research they fund be made available in open access form.

Because open access is in its infancy, it remains to be seen how it will all play out and whether open access will actually reduce the cost of scholarly publishing. Even if the cost of scholarly publishing does not drop, open access is at least making scholarly information more accessible by removing the barrier of the paywall.

The Scholarly Book Crisis

The high cost of scholarly journals has produced a crisis for scholarly books. The problem is that academic libraries have been spending such a large percentage of their collection budgets to cover the increasing cost of subscriptions to scholarly journals that they cannot afford to buy as many scholarly books as they once did, driving the sales of print-format scholarly books to historic lows.[18] A study conducted by the British Library and the Arts and Humanities Research Council found that, from 2005 to 2014, average sales of scholarly books in the United Kingdom fell from one hundred sales per title to sixty.[19] To some extent the drop in sales of print-format scholarly books is being offset by academic libraries' acquisition of scholarly books in electronic formats, but e-book acquisitions are not enough to turn around a downward trend that has been building momentum for years.

Open access publishing, however, presents an alternative that could save the scholarly book. In open access book publishing, a scholarly author whose book manuscript has been accepted for publication by a scholarly press pays an up-front fee to cover the editorial and other costs associated with creating the book. The book is then made available online at no charge, making it accessible to millions of potential readers. Readers who wish to obtain a print copy of the book can pay for an on-demand copy from the publisher. Though a growing number of scholarly publishers are experimenting with open access models for books, it remains to be seen if open access will solve the crisis in scholarly book publishing.

CHALLENGES FACING SCHOLARLY INFORMATION

While scholarly information is highly credible, it is not infallible. Perhaps the biggest challenge facing scholarly information, predatory journals, is described earlier. What follows are challenges of which anyone wishing to fully evaluate scholarly information should be aware.

Fakery Happens

While predatory journals constitute one type of fake publication, there are other variations on the theme. Between 2002 and 2005 Elsevier, the world's largest, best known, and most profitable publisher of scholarly journals, published six fake journals that were secretly sponsored by pharmaceutical companies.[20] In the digital world, it has become all too easy to pass off nonscholarly information as the real thing. In 2005 a group of MIT students created a spoofing tool called SciGen that creates what appear to be scientific papers but are really just random accumulations of words supplemented by meaningless charts and diagrams. Sadly, many papers created with SciGen have been accepted by conferences and journals that either are completely predatory or simply too lackadaisical about their editorial processes.[21]

Human Factors Come into Play

Scholars are human beings and behave as such. Scholars sometimes make mistakes. Scholars bring their baggage of personal biases with them when they interpret evidence. Both are unavoidable parts of being human. What is avoidable is resorting to such human failings as falsifying results, plagiarizing, or turning to predatory publishers—all things that (a relatively few) scholars have been known to do. Why do these few scholars cross the line? To be a scholar is to participate in a highly competitive business. When a scholar's career is at stake, the urge to take shortcuts can overwhelm even a sincere commitment to ethical behavior. It is not so much surprising that scholars occasionally cheat as it is that they do not cheat more often than they do.

Impact Factors Are Overrated

The way in which journal impact factors are used has created a number of problems. One problem is that a journal's impact factor is sometimes used as a shortcut means of evaluating the scholars who publish in that journal rather than as a way to evaluate the journal itself (the latter being the original and intended purpose of impact factors). In some fields of study, this has created an environment in which getting published in a highly rated journal becomes the overriding concern of researchers. It can reach the point where, given the choice between the following two options, researchers feel compelled to choose A over B:

A. Doing research that stands a good chance of being published in a highly ranked journal
B. Doing research that is less publishable but more likely to truly advance knowledge

Another problem arises from the fact that scholarly journals use high impact factors as justification for charging premium prices for subscriptions. In their eagerness to increase their impact factors (and income), some scholarly journals have resorted to gaming the system through what is known as "coercive citation."[22] It works like this: A scholar submits a manuscript to *Journal X*. The editors of *Journal X* say to the author, "We would like to publish your article. However, you only cite one article from *Journal X* in your manuscript. We would like you to revise your manuscript so that you cite five articles from *Journal X*." While the extra citations do nothing to improve the quality of the published article, they help increase the impact factor of *Journal X*. Similarly, scholars have been known to cite their own work as a way of driving up the number of times their articles are cited, thereby making their impact appear greater than it actually is.

Funders Influence Researchers

Scholarly researchers are constantly in search of grants to support their work, but there can be conflicts between scholarly ethics and the goals of funders. One well-known example were the scientists employed by big tobacco whose research consistently disavowed or downplayed links between smoking and diseases like cancer, heart disease, and emphysema. Similarly, there are deep concerns about the impartiality of clinical trials funded by pharmaceutical companies.[23] In the United States, the opioid epidemic that has claimed thousands of lives and has been blamed in part on the widespread overprescription of painkillers "fueled by a multifaceted campaign underwritten by pharmaceutical companies" that included funding biased research.[24] Pharmaceutical companies are not the only bad actors. Climate scientist Katherine Hayhoe has written about the conflicts she felt on learning that Exxon Corporation was spreading disinformation about climate change at the same time it was funding her climate research.[25] Another way in which funding influences research is when research funding is withheld as a way of quashing open inquiry. An example of this is when government funding agencies are ordered to stop funding certain types of research for reasons that are politically motivated.

Negative Results Are Not Sexy

If a researcher develops and tests a hypothesis but gets results that do not have the predicted content, this is called a *null result* or *negative result*. While a null result can make an important contribution to human knowledge, many journals so greatly prefer to publish positive results that publishing an article with a null result becomes almost impossible. Similarly, producing negative results is not a great way to further one's scholarly career. Experimental results that find that drug X does nothing to slow the spread of prostate cancer is simply not as exciting as results that find drug Y shows promise as an effective anticancer drug.

Peer Review Is Not Perfect

While peer review is a powerful mechanism for ensuring the quality of scholarly information, it is not a perfect mechanism. Because the referees who conduct peer review are human, they bring their biases to the table when they review the work of others. Referees may vote against the publication of research that contradicts their own work or that conflicts with mainstream thinking within their field of study. Historically, there have been cases of important articles initially being rejected by referees who failed to see the value of groundbreaking new research. In 1797, physician Edward Jenner's short paper describing his success in immunizing humans against the deadly disease smallpox was rejected by the Royal Society and went unpublished until Jenner had it published as a pamphlet at his own expense.[26] At the same time, there are cases of bogus papers being accepted because the referees did not pay sufficient (or possibly any) attention to the content of what they were reading. There have even been cases of scholars creating fake identities so that they could serve as referees for their own articles.[27] No, peer review is not broken. For the most part, it works well. But it is not infallible.

Replication Studies Are Not Valued

An important tenet of the scientific method is that experimental results must be reproducible. Replication studies are the only valid way to determine if experimental results are reproducible, but it is hard to find grant funding to carry out replication studies, many journals are reluctant to publish articles documenting replication studies, and scholars are rewarded far more for conducting new research than for carrying out replication studies.

Scholarly Information Is Misrepresented

Though scholars are not to blame for this problem, the fact is that the results of scholarly research are too often misrepresented in popular media. Scholars know that any single study can produce atypical results. Unless the results of a study have been confirmed by replication studies or have been considered in context with other studies (as is done in a systematic review), the results of any single study cannot be taken as definitive. However, when a study produces a newsworthy finding, that finding often gets reported in the media as if it were the final word on the subject. Worse, the significance of research findings is often blown out of proportion when translated from scholarly articles (which are usually very guarded in terms of any claims made) to a popular news articles (which too often overstate the significance of research findings). Whenever the results of a scholarly study are reported in the popular media, it is always a good idea to go to the original study (the primary source) and see what the original researchers have to say instead of receiving that information secondhand via popular media.

American author James Baldwin wrote, "The price one pays for pursuing any profession, or calling, is an intimate knowledge of its ugly side."[28] This is as true of the scholarly professions as of any other. However, the existence of an ugly side does not diminish all that is good about scholarly information. While not infallible, scholars form a worldwide community striving to carry out quality research and produce the most credible information possible for the benefit of people everywhere. This is both a high standard and an admirable one.

RECAP

Scholarly information is created by scholars—people who are very learned in a particular field, usually as a result of advanced education and years of study. Scholars may be academic scholars (working in higher education) or nonacademic scholars (working in private industry, for a government agency, or independently).

When scholars do research they produce scholarly information based on their research. Scholarly information can come in the form of text, images, videos, maps, data sets, sound recordings, and more. While it is common to associate research with scientists working in labs, scholars in the various fields of technology, social sciences, humanities, and the arts routinely conduct research and produce scholarly information.

The scientific method, a model for studying both the natural and the human world, is employed by scientists, technologists, and social scientists. The basic idea of the scientific method is that the acquisition of new knowledge commonly involves formulating a hypothesis, testing the hypothesis through the observation of empirical evidence, analyzing the evidence, and reaching a conclusion. Another important tenet of the scientific method is that results must be reproducible.

In order to identify scholarly information, it is important to be familiar with its most common forms:

- Scholarly journals
- Scholarly articles (which are often peer reviewed)
- Review articles

- Conference proceedings
- Scholarly monographs
- Edited scholarly books
- Textbooks
- Reference books
- Dissertations and theses
- Emerging formats: databases, software, digital maps, videos, and other digital formats

Scholarly, subject-focused databases are useful tools for locating scholarly information.

Predatory journals are a type of online publication that resemble scholarly journals but are, instead, moneymaking scams that publish substandard articles for a price. Distinguishing between legitimate scholarly journals and predatory journals can be challenging.

Money plays a role in the creation of scholarly information. The scholarly publishing industry grosses billions of dollars every year and major scholarly publishers enjoy high profit margins. In response to years of increases in the cost of scholarly information, scholars and librarians have become advocates for open access publishing, both as a way to reduce costs and as a way to make scholarly information freely available to all. Grant funding influences both who conducts research and what researchers study.

Although scholarly information constitutes, as a whole, a highly credible body of information that is essential for decision making and progress in the modern world, scholars are not infallible and the information they produce is not perfect. Being aware of the most pressing challenges that impact scholarly information is essential for evaluating scholarly information.

Help Is Where You Find It

Resources for Evaluating Information

As previous chapters have demonstrated, evaluating information is not for the faint of heart. You have to keep up your guard to make sure that you don't fall for information that seems credible but is not. Even when your guard is up, evaluating any given piece of information can take considerable time and effort; so much so that no one can thoroughly evaluate all the information they encounter and must, instead, carefully ration the time spent on evaluation. The good news is that there are information resources designed to help you check facts and/or gain perspective on an information resource's reputation for credibility.

INFORMATION WATCHDOGS

According to the nonprofit Poynter Institute for Media Studies, by June 2016 there were "more than 100 fact-checking projects active in approximately 40 countries."[1] The good news is that this means there are now many *information watchdogs* you can turn to for help in checking facts and evaluating information resources. The bad news is that keeping up with all the existing and newly emerging information watchdogs represents an ongoing challenge. Not only do you need to keep aware of what information watchdogs are out there, you need to know which of those are truly trustworthy. The fact that there are so many self-proclaimed information watchdogs means that the field is open to watchdog sites that claim to be impartial but that are, in fact, highly partisan. After all, what better way to spread lies and propaganda than by claiming to be a resolute defender of the truth, the whole truth, and nothing but the truth?

When turning to any information resource that endeavors to evaluate the credibility of other sources of information, it is good practice to learn what you can about the methodologies it uses for evaluation. Among information watchdogs, the methodologies used for evaluation are often described on an "About" page or on a separate page devoted to methodology. It is a red flag when anyone who evaluates anything fails to describe the methodologies they use for evaluation.

When checking facts, it is never a bad idea to consult more than one fact-checking resource—if second and third opinions are readily available, always seek them out. It is also important to remember that even the most reliable information watchdog may change (for the better or for the worse) over time, demonstrate occasional bias, or simply make mistakes once in a while. One of the truths about journalism is that checking facts costs money, and as a result the failure to fully check facts is often more attributable to financial considerations than it is to bias or incompetence.

A final point about information watchdogs is this: no matter how fair and impartial a watchdog may be, somebody, somewhere has blasted it as biased, unreliable, and/or in the pocket of special interests. The situation is very much like that of reviews of restaurants on public recommendation sites like Yelp—no matter how good a restaurant may be, there are always going to be at least a few negative reviews of it. Whether it is restaurants or websites that are being evaluated, your task is to look at the total picture and decide whether the praise given and the criticisms dished out are fair and reasonable.

Recognizing that no information resource is infallible or absolutely free from bias, the following resources can stake reasonable—though not irrefutable—claims as either reliable fact-checking resources or as reliable evaluators of the credibility of other information resources.

Allsides

Rather than evaluating information, Allsides presents multiple views (left, right, and center) of news stories with the goal of allowing the reader to decide what information is most credible. Allsides also rates other media outlets on a left-to-right bias scale. Funding for Allsides comes from contributions made by individuals and foundations.

Launched: 2012

Home page: www.allsides.com

About: www.allsides.com/about

American Fact Finder

Created and maintained by the US Census Bureau, American Fact Finder "provides access to data about the United States, Puerto Rico and the Island Areas." American Fact Finder is especially useful for checking facts about US populations (national, state, and local), economic conditions, health, crime, and more. The funding for American Fact Finder is provided by the US government.

Founded: 2011

Home page: factfinder.census.gov

About: www.census.gov/about/what.html

Blue Feed, Red Feed

Blue Feed, Red Feed shows unedited and unverified liberal (blue) and conservative (red) Facebook content side by side in an effort to undo the echo chamber effect in which the views of only one side are heard. Blue Feed, Red Feed is a service of the *Wall Street Journal.*

Launched: 2016

Home page: graphics.wsj.com/blue-feed-red-feed

About: graphics.wsj.com/blue-feed-red-feed/#methodology

Climate Feedback

The mission of Climate Feedback is to "help Internet users—from the general public to influential decision-makers—distinguish inaccurate climate change narratives from scientifically sound and trustworthy information in the media." The Climate Feedback team of reviewers is composed of research scientists who review popular articles on climate change, rating each article's scientific credibility. Climate Feedback is funded by the University of California, Merced; the University of California's Center for Information Research in the Interest of Society; and individual contributions.

Founded: 2015

Home page: climatefeedback.org

About: climatefeedback.org/About

Fact Checker

A feature of the *Washington Post*, Fact Checker is the work of journalist Glenn Kessler. The stated purpose of Fact Checker "is to 'truth squad' the statements of political figures regarding issues of great importance, be they national, international or local." The *Washington Post* is funded through advertising and subscription revenues and, since 2013, has been owned by Amazon CEO Jeff Bezos.

Launched: 2011

Home page: www.washingtonpost.com/news/fact-checker

About: www.washingtonpost.com/news/fact-checker/about-the-fact
   -checker

FactCheck

FactCheck bills itself as "nonpartisan, nonprofit 'consumer advocate' for voters that aims to reduce the level of deception and confusion in U.S. politics." FactCheck is supported by funding from the Annenberg Public Policy Center of the University of Pennsylvania.

Launched: 2003

Home page: www.factcheck.org

About: www.factcheck.org/about/our-mission

FiveThirtyEight

Taking its name from the number of electors in the US electoral college, FiveThirtyEight (also known as 538) uses statistical methodology to analyze public opinion and provide numerical analysis of politics, sports, science and health, economics, and culture. Founded in 2008 by statistician Nate Silver, FiveThirtyEight was affiliated with the *New York Times* from 2010 to 2012 before being acquired by ESPN.

Launched: 2008

Home page: fivethirtyeight.com

About: fivethirtyeight.com/masthead

Full Fact

Billing itself as "the UK's independent factchecking charity," Full Fact is supported by individual contributions and foundation grants, including major gifts from investor George Soros and Iranian American eBay founder Pierre Omidyar. Full Fact focuses on such UK social and political issues as the economy, international relations, health, crime, immigration, education, and law.

Launched: 2009

Home page: fullfact.org

About: fullfact.org/about

Hoax-Slayer

Hoax-Slayer is a resource for checking up on the credibility of online hoaxes, social media rumors, scams, and Internet security matters. Hoax-Slayer is supported through advertising and affiliate marketing.

Launched: 2003

Home page: www.hoax-slayer.net

About: www.hoax-slayer.net/about-this-blog

Information Is Beautiful

The mission of Information Is Beautiful is "to distill the world's data, information and knowledge into beautiful and useful graphics and diagrams." The visualizations appearing on Information Is Beautiful cover an eclectic assortment of topics ranging from media-inflamed fears to gender pay gaps to misconceptions and myths. The site is self-funded.

Founded: 2009

Home page: www.informationisbeautiful.net

About: www.informationisbeautiful.net/about

Media Bias/Fact Check

Media Bias/Fact Check uses an explicit methodology to rate other media outlets on a scale that ranges from Left Bias to Right Bias and includes such categories as "Pro-Science," "Conspiracy-Pseudoscience," "Questionable Sources," and "Satire." Media Bias/Fact Check is supported by advertising, gifts from individuals, and "the pockets of our fact checkers."

Launched: 2015

Home page: mediabiasfactcheck.com

About: mediabiasfactcheck.com/about

MedlinePlus

A service of the US National Library of Medicine, MedlinePlus offers "reliable, up-to-date health information, anytime, anywhere, for free." MedlinePlus is especially useful for fact-checking information found on commercial and nonprofit sites offering health information. The funding for MedlinePlus is provided by the US government.

Founded: 1998

Home page: medlineplus.gov

About: medlineplus.gov/aboutmedlineplus.html

OpenSecrets
OpenSecrets is the website of the Center for Responsive Politics. The mission of OpenSecrets is "tracking money in US politics and its effect on elections and public policy." OpenSecrets is supported by grants, individual contributions, licensing data, and payment for custom research.

Launched: 1996

Home page: www.opensecrets.org

About: www.opensecrets.org/about

Politifact
Run by editors and reporters from the *Tampa Bay Times*, Politifact bills itself as "a fact-checking website that rates the accuracy of claims by elected officials and others who speak up in American politics." Politifact is supported by funding from the *Tampa Bay Times*, grants, online partnerships, and advertising.

Founded: 2017

Home page: www.politifact.com

About: www.politifact.com/truth-o-meter/article/2013/nov/01/principles
  -politifact-punditfact-and-truth-o-meter

Sense about Science
UK-based Sense about Science describes itself as "an independent campaigning charity that challenges the misrepresentation of science and evidence in public life." Sense about Science is funded by gifts from individuals, scholarly societies, publishers, and foundations.

Founded: 2002

Home page: senseaboutscience.org

About: senseaboutscience.org/who-we-are

Sunlight Foundation

The mission of the Sunlight Foundation is to use "civic technology, open data, policy analysis and journalism to make our government and politics more accountable and transparent to all." For example, the Sunlight Foundation makes government information available through its "Hall of Justice" web page (hallofjustice.sunlightfoundation.com), which provides access to state and national data sets relating to criminal justice. The Sunlight Foundation is supported by gifts from private individuals and foundations.

Launched: 2006

Home page: sunlightfoundation.com

About: sunlightfoundation.com/about

Snopes

Also known as the "Urban Legends Reference Pages," Snopes addresses urban legends, Internet rumors, and stories of dubious origin. The sole source of income for Snopes comes from advertisements that appear on the website.

Launched: 1994

Home page: www.snopes.com

About: www.snopes.com/about-snopes

TruthOrFiction

TruthOrFiction describes itself as "a non-partisan website where Internet users can quickly and easily get information about e-rumors, warnings, offers, requests for help, myths, hoaxes, virus warnings, and humorous or inspirational stories that are circulated by email." TruthOrFiction tends not to focus on current events.

Launched: 1999

Home page: www.truthorfiction.com

About: www.truthorfiction.com/about-us

World Factbook

Created and maintained by the US Central Intelligence Agency, World Factbook "provides information on the history, people, government, economy, geography, communications, transportation, military, and transnational issues for 267 world entities." World Factbook also includes numerous political and geographic maps covering the entire world.

Founded: 1962

Home page: https://www.cia.gov/library/publications/resources/the -world-factbook/index.html

About: www.cia.gov/library/publications/resources/the-world-factbook/ docs/history.html

WHEN CHECKING MATTERS MOST

Recapping some points made in previous chapters, there are certain situations when making use of information watchdogs like the ones listed here is especially well advised:

- When you encounter information that plays on your emotions by making you feel especially angry, happy, fearful, vindicated, and so on.

- When you encounter information promoting conclusions that are especially outrageous, unconventional, or iconoclastic. Any information that "defies all the experts" or "changes everything" merits careful scrutiny before it can be accepted as credible.

- When the stakes are high—as when there is much to be lost if the information turns out to be noncredible—it is especially important to make sure that information is credible.

FOLLOW THE MONEY

For any information resource, but especially for those that claim to fact-check other information resources, it is worth finding out what you can about the source of funding. In the online world, you can often find information about funding sources on a site's "About" page. Any credible information resource will be up front about its sources of funding. Typically, funding for information resources comes from one or more of the following sources:

Advertisements

When an information resource is funded by advertisements, the important question to ask is, "What influence, if any, do advertisers have on the information content?" While the ideal is for advertisers to have no influence at all, that ideal is easier met in theory than in practice. For example, if an information resource carries advertisements from fast-food restaurants, can it be fully truthful when it comes to reporting anything that is critical of the fast food industry? Maybe yes. Maybe no. In either case, the question about the relationship between advertisers and credibility still needs to be asked.

Gifts

Many online information resources avoid, or at least minimize, the problem of accepting advertising dollars by instead financing their operations through gifts from individuals and foundations. While it is unlikely that an individual who contributes a few dollars a year to a favorite information resource is in a position to influence content, a wealthy individual or deep-pockets foundation that provides significant support may expect something in return. The potential influence of large gifts raises similar concerns to those raised by advertising revenue. For example, the Full Fact website described earlier is funded in part by billionaire George Soros, a major supporter of Democratic Party candidates in US elections. While it is possible for funders to take a hands-off approach that leaves content decisions to independent editors and writers, the possible influence of major donors on sites like Full Fact must certainly be taken into consideration when evaluating their credibility and impartiality.

Government Funding

It should come as no surprise that governments are quite capable of lying. This means that it is perfectly reasonable to ask if politics could influence the content of government-supported information resources. World Factbook (mentioned earlier) is a perfect example, seeing that it is funded by the US Central Intelligence Agency—an organization with a long history of playing fast and loose with the truth. In its defense, because World Factbook presents nonclassified information that is largely statistical in nature (such as population, economic, and geographic data), its sponsorship by a clandestine intelligence organization is not as problematic as if World Factbook were presenting subjective information that is more susceptible to politically motivated manipulation. An important distinction to make when evaluating government-supported information resources is the difference between information resources produced by government agencies in fulfillment of their official missions (such as the information provided by the Census Bureau or the National Institutes of Health) versus overtly political sources of government information (such as the web pages of elected officials). While the former may or may not be influenced by political considerations, the latter are, by their very nature, entirely political.

FIGHTING THE SPREAD OF FAKE NEWS

A number of initiatives have been launched in recent years to fight the spread of noncredible information, many surfacing in the wake of the furor over fake news that erupted in the latter half of 2016. While it is unlikely that such efforts can entirely eliminate fake news, the question remains, "Do these initiatives have the potential to push back on the problem of fake news and, more broadly, the spread of information that is simply not credible?"

Emerging Efforts

One example of emerging efforts to fight fake news is the April 2017 pledge of the philanthropic investment firm Omidyar Network to donate $100 million over three years for the purpose of "supporting independent media, tackling misinformation and hate speech, and looking at ways in which technology can help repair relationships between citizens and government."[2] Similarly, and at approximately the same time, Jimmy Wells, the founder of *Wikipedia*, announced plans to launch Wikitribune, a project to pair experienced journalists with volunteer amateurs for the purpose of creating a credible, factually based, ad-free source for news.[3]

Social Media

A number of social media outlets (see figure 8.1) have taken blame for their role as conduits of fake news. In response to criticism from individuals, politicians, and (perhaps most persuasively) major advertisers, such social media outlets as Facebook, YouTube, and Twitter have promised to take steps to reduce fake news on social media:

- Shortly after the US elections of 2016, Facebook CEO Mark Zuckerberg promised that Facebook would institute measures to combat the proliferation of fake news.[4]
- In 2017, both Google and Bing began adding "fact check" tags to stories that have been judged truthful by multiple news publishers and fact-checking organizations.[5]
- Also in 2017, Twitter began looking for ways to allow its users to flag fake news.[6]

Whether these or other efforts will succeed remains to be seen. Both Google and Facebook failed a major test of their abilities to fight fake news in October 2017 when they posted fake news regarding the Las Vegas Strip shooting alongside reports from credible information sources.[7] Realistically, social media outlets face formidable financial and practical hurdles if they are to fight fake news. Besides staying afloat financially, any social media outlets wishing to stem the proliferation of fake news must confront the complexity and nuance of what does or does not constitute fake news while avoiding actions that reflect either partisanship or censorship.

AI Solutions?

Could technology, in the form of machine learning tools or straight-up artificial intelligence (AI), solve the problem of separating credible information from noncredible information? Some are trying that approach. In November 2016, Google provided funding to Full Fact (described earlier) to develop automated fact-checking software.[8] In August 2017 journalists began trying out the Full Fact fact-checking software, quickly discovering it to be somewhat fallible in the early stage of its development.[9] While it is likely that automated fact-checking software will improve over time, there are strong arguments that artificial intelligence will never become good enough at negotiating the

FIGURE 8.1
Popular social media outlets. *istock/543077374*

nuances of language, data, and opinion to fully automate the task of evaluating information.[10]

RECAP

Information watchdogs can be helpful to anyone seeking to evaluate information. However, they are not a cure-all for fake news and noncredible information, and the same caveats apply to information watchdogs as apply to the information sources they strive to evaluate. Awareness of fake news has led to the emergence of new initiatives to push back against fake news as well as attempts to use advanced technology to help people identify noncredible information. The newness of such efforts, coupled with the complexity of evaluating information, means that their ultimate success or failure remains to be seen.

Final Thoughts

As the United States was expanding westward during the second half of the nineteenth century, various pseudoscientists, land speculators, and politicians promoted the unproven theory that "rain follows the plow."[1] Their reasoning (or lack thereof) held that cultivating the arid lands lying west of the one hundredth meridian would bring the rain necessary to raise the types of crops grown farther east. By simply applying the plow to the dry soil of the West, so the advocates' reasoning went, farmers would initiate an annual cycle of snowy winters and rainy summers equivalent to those experienced in states like Iowa, Illinois, and Indiana. The evidence supporting this argument was based on a few exceptionally wet years that happened to coincide with the early stages of westward migration. This, along with large doses of unbridled optimism and pure greed, was all it took to get the ball rolling.

"We tend to accept information that confirms our prior beliefs and ignore or discredit information that does not. This confirmation bias settles over our eyes like distorting spectacles for everything we look at."

—*Kyle Hill, science writer*[2]

The idea that rain follows the plow proved to be an extremely appealing notion in a United States that was eagerly expanding westward. After all, wasn't it America's manifest destiny to settle the continent from coast to coast? And wasn't the yeoman farmer—each man independently working his own plot of land—the keystone of Jeffersonian democracy? And weren't there millions of square miles of the "Great American Desert" waiting to be turned into prosperous, rain-nourished farms? Hearing all these questions answered with a resounding "Yes," Congress passed the Homestead Act of 1862, thereby granting individuals the right to claim 160 acres of western land on which to establish freestanding farms.

"Democracy must be built through open societies that share information. When there is information, there is enlightenment. When there is debate, there are solutions."

—*Atifete Jahjaga, former president of Kosovo*[3]

Not everyone, however, bought into the idea that cultivating western soil would cause the desert to bloom. John Wesley Powell, a geologist and government official who had actually explored the western United States, was one such naysayer. In his book *Report on the Land of the Arid Regions of the United States*, Powell argued that only the small percentage of western lands adjacent to reliable water sources were suitable for agriculture without the construction of major irrigation systems.[4] Though Powell's ideas about the best ways to sustainably develop the West were not entirely correct, they were far more correct than the notions of his opponents. Most of the western United States was, and remains, too arid for the type of agriculture practiced east of the one hundredth meridian, plowing the ground did nothing to make the rain fall any harder, and thousands of homesteaders ended up going bust in spite of the years of backbreaking labor they put into their claims. The impoverished Dust Bowl refugees who fled their dried-up farms in the 1930s were just one example of those who paid a high price for a nation's badly informed choices. In the twenty-first century, the United States is still dealing with a host of economic, social, and environmental problems resulting, either directly or indirectly, from the entirely unsupported belief that rain follows the plow.

"For if the premise upon which our pluralistic society rests, which as I understand it is that if the people are given sufficient undiluted information, they will then somehow, even after long, sober second thoughts, reach the right conclusion. If that premise is wrong, then not only the corporate image but the corporations and the rest of us are done for."

—*Edward R. Murrow, journalist*[5]

It is easy to look back with a knowing smile at those gullible enough to believe that the act of plowing the ground could make it rain. But the truth is that the people who evaluated the proposition that rain follows the plow faced essentially the same sort of information dilemma faced by people living today. On one hand, there was information supporting the idea that working the soil would bring rain; on the other, there was information supporting the opposite point of view. And because there are always more than two sides to every controversy, there was information that fell between the extremes. It was up to the people of that time to choose which information was most credible. In the end, they chose poorly.

"We're not that much smarter than we used to be, even though we have much more information—and that means the real skill now is learning how to pick out the useful information from all this noise."

—*Nate Silver, statistician and founder of FiveThirtyEight*[6]

The story of rain follows the plow is a cautionary tale of how misinformation can lead to bad decisions. People in the Digital Age must make decisions on complex matters ranging from climate change to public health to personal finance to food choices. The one big difference between the present and the past is the vastly larger amount of information that exists today and the lightning speed at which information travels.

"Information sharing. That's what the Internet was designed for; it's what it does best. People's lives improve and humankind makes progress when we share our best ideas and others can act on them. This overwhelms all the bad stuff."

—*Vint Cerf, computer scientist and Internet pioneer*[7]

In the Digital Age, the quantity of information and speed at which it travels can be overwhelming. Some have coped with this reality by descending into a downward spiral of cynicism in which all information is dismissed as a lie, as elements of a vast conspiracy to make fools of us all. Some have coped by giving up on genuinely caring whether information is credible or not, choosing to accept whatever information suits their mood as casually as they might pick videos off a streaming service or songs from a playlist. While the adoption of these or similar "post-truth" coping mechanisms may seem like exercises of free will or affirmations of individualism, the end result is more akin to being set adrift than being set free. Human beings require information—imperfect as it may be—to form rational opinions and make the best possible decisions, both as individuals and as members of a society.

"When the world throws you too much information, the only way you can stay sane or survive is to look for pattern recognition. Amidst all the blurs, is there a constellation that emerges, is there a straight line that's emerging?"

—*Douglas Coupland, author and artist*[8]

To not give up requires effort. But even with effort, evaluating information can be frustrating. There will be times when deciding where the truth really lies becomes all but impossible, when the pursuit of the truth leads to dead ends. There will be times when your skills for evaluating information let you down, when a fact or journal article or news story that passed your best credibility tests turns out to be not much more than a blatant lie. But this is the nature of working with that tricky, often slippery substance called *information*. When your attempt to evaluate information goes wrong, you learn what you can from the experience and try to do better next time. Unless we are to put the fates of ourselves and our societies at the mercy of purveyors (both intentional and unintentional) of misleading information, it is our duty to care about credibility and to practice due diligence in evaluating the information we encounter, share, and create.

"The key to good decision making is evaluating the available information— the data—and combining it with your own estimates of pluses and minuses."

—*Emily Oster, economist*[9]

Notes

PREFACE

1. Paul G. Zurkowski, "The Information Service Environment Relationships and Priorities. Related Paper No. 5" (Washington, DC: National Commission on Libraries and Information Science, 1974), files.eric.ed.gov/fulltext/ED100391.pdf.

2. Mary F. Salony, "The History of Bibliographic Instruction: Changing Trends from Books to the Electronic World," *Reference Librarian* 24, nos. 51–52 (1995): 31–51, doi:10.1300/J120v24n51_06.

3. Najmabadi Shannon, "Information Literacy—It's Become a Priority in an Era of Fake News," *Chronicle of Higher Education*, February 26, 2017, www.chronicle.com/article/Information-Literacy/239264.

4. Donald A. Barclay, "The Challenge Facing Libraries in an Era of Fake News," *Conversation*, January 2017, theconversation.com/the-challenge-facing-libraries-in-an-era-of-fake-news-70828.

CHAPTER 1

1. Faiz Siddiqui and Susan Svrluga, "N.C. Man Told Police He Went to D.C. Pizzeria with Gun to Investigate Conspiracy Theory," *Washington Post*, December 5, 2016, www.washingtonpost.com/news/local/wp/2016/12/04/d-c-police-respond-to-report-of-a-man-with-a-gun-at-comet-ping-pong-restaurant/?utm_term=.37de81332599.

2. United States Surgeon General's Advisory Committee on Smoking and Health, United States Public Health Service, *Smoking and Health: Report of the Advisory Committee to the Surgeon General of the Public Health Service* (Washington, DC: US Government Printing Office, 1964), books.google.com/books?id=yPtqAAAAMAAJ.

3. Richard Kluger, *Ashes to Ashes—America's Hundred-Year Cigarette War, the Public Health, and the Unabashed Triumph of Philip Morris* (New York: Alfred A. Knopf, 1996), 260.

4. CDC's Office on Smoking and Health, "Trends in Current Cigarette Smoking among High School Students and Adults, United States, 1965–2014," Centers for Disease Control and Prevention, 2014, www.cdc.gov/tobacco/data_statistics/tables/trends/cig_smoking/.

5. Ahmed Jamal et al., "Current Cigarette Smoking Among Adults—United States, 2005–2014," *Morbidity and Mortality Weekly Report (MMWR)* 64, no. 44 (2015): 1233–40, www.cdc.gov/mmwr/preview/mmwrhtml/mm6444a2.htm.

6. Stanford University and Center for the Study of Language and Information (U.S.), *Stanford Encyclopedia of Philosophy* (Stanford: Stanford University, 1997), plato.stanford.edu/entries/practical-reason/.

7. Martin Fleischmann and Stanley Pons, "Electrochemically Induced Nuclear Fusion of Deuterium," *Journal of Electroanalytical Chemistry and Interfacial Electrochemistry* 261, no. 2 (1989): 301–8. doi:dx.doi.org/10.1016/0022-0728(89)80006-3.

8. "US Police Shootings: How Many Die Each Year?" BBC News, accessed June 8, 2017, www.bbc.com/news/magazine-36826297.

9. National Aeronautics and Space Administration, *The Apollo 11 Telemetry Data Recordings: A Final Report*, 2009, www.hq.nasa.gov/alsj/a11/Apollo_11_TV_Tapes_Report.pdf.

10. Tim Weiner, "W. Mark Felt, Watergate Deep Throat, Dies at 95," *New York Times*, December 19, 2008, www.nytimes.com/2008/12/19/washington/19felt.html.

11. Tor Halmrast, "Tune In to ISO 16 ! The Long and Oscillating History of Standard Tuning Frequency," *ISO Focus +: The Magazine of the International Organization for Standardization*, 2012, 25–27, http://tor.halmrast.no/HistoryTuningPitch%20ISO16.pdf.

12. Michael J. Hayde, *My Name's Friday: The Unauthorized but True Story of Dragnet and the Films of Jack Webb* (Nashville: Cumberland House, 2001), 72–73.

13. William W. Fitzhugh and Elisabeth I. Ward, *Vikings: The North Atlantic Saga* (Washington, DC: Smithsonian Institution Press in Association with the National Museum of Natural History, 2000).

14. *The Trial of William Wemms, James Hartegan, William M'Cauley, Hugh White, Matthew Killroy, William Warren, John Carrol, and Hugh Montgomery: Soldiers in His Majesty's 29th Regiment of Foot, for the Murder of Crispus Attucks, Samuel Gray, Samuel Maverick* (Boston, MA: Printed by J. Flemming, 1770).

15. *Treason Unmask'd: or the Queen's Title, the Revolution, and the Hanover Succession. Against the Treasonable Positions, of a Book Lately Publish'd, Intitled, The Hereditary Right of the Crown of England Asserted; the History of the Succession Since the Conquest Clear'd, and the True English Constitution Vindicated, from the Misrepresentations of Dr. Higden's View.* 1713. London: printed, and sold by the booksellers of London and Westminster, 255.

16. "The Republicans in New Orleans; Reagan's Address: Hailing Fruits of the Party's Dream of 1980," *New York Times*, August 16, 1988.

17. Except that the greatest baseball player of all time was, in fact, Willie Mays. Everybody knows that.

18. Liam Stack and Christina Anderson, "Sweden's Defense and National Security Adviser? 'We Don't Know This Guy,'" *New York Times*, February 27, 2017, www .nytimes.com/2017/02/26/world/europe/sweden-fraud-fox-news-commentator-trump.html?mtrref=www.google.com&gwh=067C9C63DCADDB05036AB2AEFFE7 E46B&gwt=pay.

19. Will Rogers, "From Nuts to the Soup," *New York Times*, August 31, 1924.

20. The Idaho Spud candy bar is delicious. You really need to try one if you never have.

CHAPTER 2

1. Claire Wardle, "Fake News. It's Complicated.," FirstDraft, 2017, firstdraftnews .com/fake-news-complicated/.

2. Hunt Allcott and Matthew Gentzkow, "Social Media and Fake News in the 2016 Election," *Journal of Economic Perspectives* 31, no. 2 (2017): 211–36, www.aeaweb .org/full_issue.php?doi=10.1257/jep.31.2#page=213.

3. Don Tynan, "How Facebook Powers Money Machines for Obscure Political 'News' Sites," *Guardian*, August 24, 2016.

4. Scott Pelly, "How Fake News Becomes a Popular, Trending Topic," *60 Minutes*, 2017, www.cbsnews.com/news/how-fake-news-find-your-social-media-feeds/.

5. Javier C. Hernandez, "Chinese Mistake Satire on Trump for Real News," *New York Times*, March 8, 2017, www.nytimes.com/2017/03/08/world/asia/china-trump -media-satire.html?_r=0.

6. Karl E. Meyer, "The Editorial Notebook–Trenchcoats, Then and Now," *New York Times*, June 24, 1990, www.nytimes.com/1990/06/24/opinion/the-editorial -notebook-trenchcoats-then-and-now.html.

7. Leslie Jones, "The German-Jewish Soldiers of the First World War," *History Today*, June 2013, www.historytoday.com/blog/2013/06/german-jewish-soldiers -first-world-war.

8. Alec MacGillis, "Penn State's Post-Sandusky Public Relations Repair Gets a Helping Hand," *New Republic*, February 2014, newrepublic.com/article/116766/ penn-states-post-sandusky-public-relations-repair-gets-helping-hand.

9. "Stanford Research into the Impact of Tobacco Advertising," accessed June 16, 2017, tobacco.stanford.edu/tobacco_main/exhibit.php?token=fm_museum_mt044 .php.

10. Examples of cigarette "cast ads" can still be viewed on YouTube: Slightlymentholated, "Beverly Hillbillies—Cast Ad #03—Winston Cigarettes," YouTube video, August 3, 2008, www.youtube.com/watch?v=xEx44ETP8Ac; Brunoreo, "Flintstones Winston Cigarettes Commercial," YouTube video, June 19, 2006, www.youtube.com/watch?v=FqdTBDkUEEQ.

11. James D Sargent, Jennifer J. Tickle, Michael L. Beach, Madeline A. Dalton, M. Bridget Ahrens, and Todd F. Heatherton, "Brand Appearances in Contemporary Cinema Films and Contribution to Global Marketing of Cigarettes," *Lancet* 357, no. 9249 (January 2001): 29–32, doi:10.1016/S0140-6736(00)03568-6.

12. Joe B. Tye, Kenneth E. Warner, and Stanton A. Glantz, "Tobacco Advertising and Consumption: Evidence of a Causal Relationship," *Journal of Public Health Policy* 8, no. 4 (1987): 492–508, www.jstor.org/stable/3342275.

13. "Our First 10 Years," BBC News, 2007, news.bbc.co.uk/2/hi/in _depth/629/629/7057140.stm.

14. Frank M. O'Brien, *The Story of the Sun: New York, 1833–1918* (New York: George H. Doran, 1918), 64–101, hdl.handle.net/2027/miun.agd0447.0001.001?urlap pend=%3Bseq=80.

15. Patrick E. Tyler and Lewis M. Simons, "'Jimmy' Episode Evokes Outrage, Sadness," *Washington Post*, April 17, 1981, https://www.washingtonpost.com/ archive/politics/1981/04/17/jimmy-episode-evokes-outrage-sadness/531a6b43-0d49 -40f0-800a-17624bac25c9/?utm_term=.6c06a203d8d9.

16. Cary D. Adkinson, "The Amazing Spider-Man and the Evolution of the Comics Code: A Case Study in Cultural Criminology," *Journal of Criminal Justice and Popular Culture* 15, no. 3 (2008): 241–61.

17. Allcott and Gentzkow, "Social Media and Fake News in the 2016 Election," 232.

18. Brooke Kroeger and Cary Abrams, "Anatomy of the Great Banana-Smoking Hoax of 1967," *East Village Other*, 2017, localeastvillage.com/2012/02/18/anatomy -of-the-great-banana-smoking-hoax-of-1967/.

19. Felix Kessler, "Light Up a Banana: Students Bake Peels to Kick Up Their Heels," *Wall Street Journal*, March 30, 1967.

20. William H. Dutton, "Fake News, Echo Chambers and Filter Bubbles: Underresearched and Overhyped," *Conversation*, May 2017, theconversation .com/fake-news-echo-chambers-and-filter-bubbles-underresearched-and- overhyped-76688.

21. James R Lewis, "Satanic Ritual Abuse," in *The Oxford Handbook of New Religious Movements*, ed. James R. Lewis and Inga B. Tollefsen, vol. 2 (New York: Oxford University Press, 2016), 210–21.

22. "The Size of the World Wide Web (the Internet)," WorldWideWebSize.com, 2017, www.worldwidewebsize.com/.

23. "Twitter: Number of Active Users 2010–2017. Statista," Statista, 2017, www .statista.com/statistics/282087/number-of-monthly-active-twitter-users/.

24. Seth Fiegerman, "Facebook Tops 1.9 Billion Monthly Users–May. 3, 2017," CNNtech, 2017, money.cnn.com/2017/05/03/technology/facebook-earnings/index.html.

25. John Harrison, *The Library of Isaac Newton* (Cambridge: Cambridge University Press, 1978), 286.

26. Eugene R. Hanson, "College Libraries: The Colonial Period to the Twentieth Century," *Advances in Library Administration and Organization* 8 (1989): 171–172, 99.

27. Winton U. Solberg, "Edmund Janes James Builds a Library: The University of Illinois Library, 1904–1920," *Libraries & Culture* 39, no. 1 (2004): 36–37, 75.

28. "Facts and Figures: UC Libraries," University of California Libraries, 2017, libraries.universityofcalifornia.edu/about/facts-and-figures.

29. Carla Marinucci, "Doctored Kerry Photo Brings Anger, Threat of Suit/Software, Net Make It Easy to Warp Reality," *San Francisco Chronicle*, February 20, 2004.

30. Sebastian Anthony, "Adobe Demos 'Photoshop for Audio,' Lets You Edit Speech as Easily as Text," arsTechnica, 2016, arstechnica.com/information-technology/2016/11/adobe-voco-photoshop-for-audio-speech-editing/.

31. Bence Kollanyi, Philip N. Howard, and Samuel C. Woolley, "Bots and Automation over Twitter during the First US Presidential Debate," 2016, 1, assets.documentcloud.org/documents/3144967/Trump-Clinton-Bots-Data.pdf.

32. Caitlin Dewey, "One in Four Debate Tweets Comes from a Bot. Here's How to Spot Them.," *Washington Post*, October 19, 2016, www.washingtonpost.com/news/the-intersect/wp/2016/10/19/one-in-four-debate-tweets-comes-from-a-bot-heres-how-to-spot-them/?utm_term=.9297567b6d49.

33. "Botometer by OSoMe," Botometer, accessed June 20, 2017, botometer.iuni.iu.edu/#!/.

34. Klint Finley, "This News-Writing Bot Is Now Free for Everyone," *Wired*, October 2015, www.wired.com/2015/10/this-news-writing-bot-is-now-free-for-everyone/.

35. Jonathan Hochman, "What Is Search Engine Optimization Manipulation?" *National Law Review*, May 2016, www.natlawreview.com/article/what-search-engine-optimization-manipulation.

CHAPTER 3

1. Videos demonstrating the glowing soda-pop trick can still be found on YouTube and other sites, though by now they have been identified as fakes by commentators.

2. "Glurge–TV Tropes," TV Tropes, accessed June 23, 2017, tvtropes.org/pmwiki/ pmwiki.php/Main/Glurge.

3. Kimberly L Barrett, "Exploring Community Levels of Lead (Pb) and Youth Violence," *Sociological Spectrum*, June 16, 2017, 1–18, doi:10.1080/02732173.2017.1 319307.

4. Bill Nye, *Bill Nye's History of the United States* (Chicago: Thompson & Thomas, 1894), file://catalog.hathitrust.org/Record/006251512.

5. Frank M. O'Brien, *The Story of the Sun. New York, 1833–1918* (New York: George H. Doran Company, 1918), 64–101.

6. Mary Grace Garis, "Marilyn Monroe Misquotations: A Brief Overview," *Elle*, 2014, www.elle.com/culture/celebrities/a15424/marilyn-monroe-misquotations/.

7. Albert Einstein, "On the Electrodynamics of Moving Bodies [Zur Elektrodynamik Bewegter Körper]," *Annalen Der Physik* 17, no. 10 (1905): 891–921, einsteinpapers.press.princeton.edu/vol2-trans/154.

8. "'Hitler's Last Birthday'," *New York Times*, April 21, 1944.

9. Samantha Grossman, "Making a Murderer: Here's the Evidence That Was Left Out," *Time*, January 2016, time.com/4167699/netflix-making-a-murderer-evidence-left-out/.

10. Elizabeth F. Loftus, *Eyewitness Testimony* (Harvard University Press, 1996).

11. "The Amazing, Untrue Story of a September 11 Survivor," National Public Radio, 2012, www.npr.org/2012/04/14/149399210/the-amazing-untrue-story-of-a -sept-11-survivor.

12. Derek Bok, *Higher Education in America* (Princeton, NJ: Princeton University Press, 2013).

13. Lynn Hasher, David Goldstein, and Thomas Toppino, "Frequency and the Conference of Referential Validity," *Journal of Verbal Learning and Verbal Behavior* 16, no. 1 (1977): 107–12.

14. Josh Quittner, "The War between Alt.tasteless and Rec.pets.cats," *Wired*, May 1994, www.wired.com/1994/05/alt-tasteless/.

15. Justin Kruger and David Dunning, "Unskilled and Unaware of It: How Difficulties in Recognizing One's Own Incompetence Lead to Inflated Self-Assessments," *Journal of Personality and Social Psychology* 77, no. 6 (1999): 1121–34.

16. Khalid Mahmood, "Do People Overestimate Their Information Literacy Skills? A Systematic Review of Empirical Evidence on the Dunning-Kruger Effect," *Communications in Information Literacy* 10, no. 2 (2016): 199–213.

CHAPTER 5

1. Michael E. Ruane, "Alexander Gardner: The Mysteries of the Civil War's Photographic Giant," *Washington Post*, December 23, 2011, www.washingtonpost .com/local/alexander-gardner-the-mysteries-of-the-civil-wars-photographic -giant/2011/12/12/gIQAptHhDP_story.html?utm_term=.bf027afba0c0.

2. *Wikipedia*, s.v. "Wikipedia: Protection Policy," en.wikipedia.org/wiki/ Wikipedia:Protection_policy, accessed July 26, 2017.

CHAPTER 6

1. Joel Best, *Damned Lies and Statistics: Untangling Numbers from the Media, Politicians, and Activists*, updated ed. (Berkeley: University of California Press, 2012), 1–4.

2. Centers for Disease Control and Prevention, "WISQARS (Web-Based Injury Statistics Query and Reporting System) | Injury Center | CDC," www.cdc.gov/ injury/wisqars/index.html, accessed August 2, 2017.

3. Mary DeYoung, "A Painted Devil: Constructing the Satanic Ritual Abuse of Children Problem," *Aggression and Violent Behavior* 1, no. 3 (1996): 235–48.

4. Michael Schroeder, "Enron Debacle Spurs Calls for Controls," *Wall Street Journal*, Eastern edition, December 14, 2001.

5. Michael Teitelbaum and Jay Winter, "Why People Fight So Much About the Census," *Washington Post*, August 30, 1998, www.washingtonpost.com/wp-srv/ politics/daily/aug98/census30.htm.

6. Pervill Squire, "Why the 1936 *Literary Digest* Poll Failed," *Public Opinion Quarterly* 52, no. 1 (1988): 125–33. doi:doi.org/10.1086/269085.

7. Centers for Disease Control and Prevention, "WISQARS."

8. Lauren Averett Byers and Charles M. Rudin, "Small Cell Lung Cancer: Where Do We Go from Here?" *Cancer* 121, no. 5 (March 1, 2015): 664–72. doi:10.1002/cncr.29098.

9. World Health Organization, "Road Traffic Deaths and Proportion of Road Users by Country/Area Country/Area General," 2015, www.who.int/violence _injury_prevention/road_safety_status/2015/TableA2.pdf?ua=1.

10. Centers for Disease Control and Prevention, "Motor Vehicle Crash Deaths | VitalSigns | CDC," 2016, www.cdc.gov/vitalsigns/motor-vehicle-safety/index.html.

11. Centers for Disease Control and Prevention, "Motor Vehicle Crash Deaths."

12. Centers for Disease Control and Prevention, "Motor Vehicle Crash Deaths."

13. Leo Kanner, "Autistic Disturbances of Affective Contact," *Nervous Child* 2, no. 3 (1943): 217–50. mail.neurodiversity.com/library_kanner_1943.pdf.

14. Lorna Wing and David Potter, "The Epidemiology of Autistic Spectrum Disorders: Is the Prevalence Rising?" *Developmental Disabilities Research Reviews* 8, no. 3 (2002): 151–61.

CHAPTER 7

1. Ellie Bothwell, "University Researchers Key 'in 40% of Top Inventions Since 1950s,'" *Times Higher Education*, May 21, 2017, www.timeshighereducation.com/news/university-researchers-key-40-top-inventions-1950s.

2. Caroline Nicholson, Julienne Meyer, Mary Flatley, and Cheryl Holman, "The Experience of Living at Home with Frailty in Old Age: A Psychosocial Qualitative Study," *International Journal of Nursing Studies* 50, no. 9 (2013): 1172–79.

3. Zahra Ebrahimi, Synneve Dahlin-Ivanoff, Kajsa Eklund, Annika Jakobsson, and Katarina Wilhelmson, "Self-Rated Health and Health-Strengthening Factors in Community-Living Frail Older People," *Journal of Advanced Nursing* 71, no. 4 (2015): 825–36.

4. Xin Gu and Karen L Blackmore, "Recent Trends in Academic Journal Growth," *Scientometrics* 108, no. 2 (August 2016): 693–716. doi:10.1007/s11192-016-1985-3.

5. Ramya H. Tunuguntla, Robert Y Henley, Yun-Chiao Yao, Tuan Anh Pham, Meni Wanunu, and Aleksandr Noy, "Enhanced Water Permeability and Tunable Ion Selectivity in Subnanometer Carbon Nanotube Porins," *Science* 357, no. 6353 (2017): 792–96. doi:10.1126/science.aan2438.

6. Alessandra Potenza, "These Microscopic Tubes May One Day Help Turn Seawater to Drinking Water," The Verge, August 2017, www.theverge .com/2017/8/24/16189762/drinkable-seawater-carbon-nanotubes-water-filters -aquaporins.

7. Ewen Callaway, "Publishing Elite Turns against Impact Factor," *Nature* 535 (2016): 210–11, www.nature.com/polopoly_fs/1.20224.1468429701!/menu/main/ topColumns/topLeftColumn/pdf/nature.2016.20224.pdf?origin=ppub.

8. Heather Piwowar, "Altmetrics: Value All Research Products," *Nature* 493, no. 7431 (2013): 159, eprints.icrisat.ac.in/12069/1/value-all-research-products.pdf.

9. Paul Basken, "Why Beall's List Died—and What It Left Unresolved about Open Access," *Chronicle of Higher Education*, September 12, 2017.

10. Rick Anderson, "Cabell's New Predatory *Journal Blacklist*: A Review," *Scholarly Kitchen*, July 2017, scholarlykitchen.sspnet.org/2017/07/25/cabells-new-predatory -journal-blacklist-review/.

11. Tom Spears, "How My Fake Science Paper Earned Me a Shot at an Editor's Job," *Ottawa Citizen*, November 24, 2014, ottawacitizen.com/news/local-news/ok -no-problem-fakery-is-fine-at-bottom-feeding-journal.

12. Thomas C. Chalmers, "Effects of Ascorbic Acid on the Common Cold: An Evaluation of the Evidence," *American Journal of Medicine* 58, no. 4 (1975): 532–36.

13. Jorge Cauz, "*Encyclopædia Britannica*'s President on Killing Off a 244-Year-Old Product," *Harvard Business Review* 91, no. 3 (2013): 39–42.

14. Jennifer Lin and Martin Fenner, "Altmetrics in Evolution: Defining and Redefining the Ontology of Article-Level Metrics," *Information Standards Quarterly* 25, no. 2 (2013): 20–26.

15. Bo-Christer Björk, "Scholarly Journal Publishing in Transition—from Restricted to Open Access," *Electronic Markets* 27, no. 2 (2017): 101–9.

16. Vincent Larivière, Stefanie Haustein, and Philippe Mongeon, "The Oligopoly of Academic Publishers in the Digital Era," *PloS One* 10, no. 6 (2015): e0127502. doi:doi.org/10.1371/journal.pone.0127502.

17. PubMed Central, accessed August 26, 2017, www.ncbi.nlm.nih.gov/pmc.

18. Donald A. Barclay, "Academic Print Books Are Dying. What's the Future?" *Conversation*, 2015, theconversation.com/academic-print-books-are-dying-whats -the-future-46248.

19. Michael Jubb, *Academic Books and Their Futures: A Report to the AHRC and the British Library, London* (London, 2017). academicbookfuture.files.wordpress .com/2017/06/academic-books-and-their-futures_jubb1.pdf.

20. Bob Grant, "Elsevier Published 6 Fake Journals," *Scientist*, May 2009, www.the -scientist.com/?articles.view/articleNo/27383/title/Elsevier-published-6-fake -journals.

21. Alan Burdick, "'Paging Dr. Fraud': The Fake Publishers That Are Ruining Science," *New Yorker*, March 2017, www.newyorker.com/tech/elements/paging-dr -fraud-the-fake-publishers-that-are-ruining-science.

22. Allen W. Wilhite and Eric A. Fong, "Coercive Citation in Academic Publishing," *Science* 335, no. 6068 (2012): 542–43.

23. Emmanuel Stamatakis, Richard Weiler, and John Ioannidis, "Undue Industry Influences That Distort Healthcare Research, Strategy, Expenditure and Practice: A Review," *European Journal of Clinical Investigation* 43, no. 5 (2013): 469–75.

24. Andrew Kolodny, "The Opioid Epidemic in 6 Charts," *Conversation*, October 2017. theconversation.com/the-opioid-epidemic-in-6-charts-81601.

25. Katherine Hayhoe, "I Was an Exxon-Funded Climate Scientist," *Conversation*, August 24, 2017, theconversation.com/i-was-an-exxon-funded-climate -scientist-49855.

26. Stefan Riedel, "Edward Jenner and the History of Smallpox and Vaccination," *Proceedings (Baylor University. Medical Center)* 18, no. 1 (January 2005): 21–25, www.ncbi.nlm.nih.gov/pubmed/16200144.

27. Cat Ferguson, Adam Marcus, and Ivan Oransky, "The Peer-Review Scam," *Nature* 515, no. 7528 (2014): 480.

28. James Baldwin, "The Black Boy Looks at the White Boy," in *The Price of the Ticket: Collected Nonfiction 1948–1985* (New York: St. Martin's Press, 1985), 302.

CHAPTER 8

1. Alexios Mantzarlis, "There's Been an Explosion of International Fact-Checkers, but They Face Big Challenges," Poynter, 2016, www.poynter.org/news/theres-been -explosion-international-fact-checkers-they-face-big-challenges.

2. Anita Singh, "eBay Founder Pierre Omidyar Commits $100M to Fight 'Fake News' and Hate Speech," *Telegraph*, April 5, 2017, www.telegraph.co.uk/ news/2017/04/04/ebay-founder-pierre-omidyar-commits-100m-fight-fake-news -hate/.

3. "*Wikipedia*'s Jimmy Wales Creates News Service Wikitribune," BBC News, 2017, www.bbc.com/news/technology-39695767.

4. Mike Isaac, "Facebook Considering Ways to Combat Fake News, Mark Zuckerberg Says," *New York Times*, November 19, 2016, https://www.nytimes .com/2016/11/20/business/media/facebook-considering-ways-to-combat-fake-news -mark-zuckerberg-says.html.

5. Jacob Kastrenakes, "Bing Now Shows Fact Checks in Search Results," The Verge, 2017, www.theverge.com/2017/9/16/16318924/bing-fact-check-label-added -search-results.

6. Elizabeth Dwoskin, "Twitter Is Looking for Ways to Let Users Flag Fake News, Offensive Content," *Washington Post*, June 29, 2017, www.washingtonpost.com/ news/the-switch/wp/2017/06/29/twitter-is-looking-for-ways-to-let-users-flag-fake -news/?utm_term=.d534f61b96fb.

7. David Pierson, "Facebook and Google Pledged to Stop Fake News. So Why Did They Promote Las Vegas-Shooting Hoaxes?" *Los Angeles Times*, October 2, 2017, www.latimes.com/business/la-fi-tn-vegas-fake-news-20171002-story.html.

8. Caroline Mortimer, "Google Funds Automated Fact-Checking Software in Bid to Fight Fake News," *Independent*, November 17, 2016, www.independent.co.uk/ life-style/gadgets-and-tech/news/google-fake-news-fight-facebook-fact-check -fullfact-a7422861.html.

9. Robert Booth, "Journalists to Use 'Immune System' Software against Fake News," *Guardian*, August 8, 2017, www.theguardian.com/technology/2017/aug/08/ fake-news-full-fact-software-immune-system-journalism-soros-omidyar.

10. Tom Simonite, "Humans Can't Expect AI to Just Fight Fake News for Them," *Wired*, June 2017, www.wired.com/story/fake-news-challenge-artificial-intelligence.

FINAL THOUGHTS

1. Wallace Stegner, *Beyond the Hundredth Meridian: John Wesley Powell and the Second Opening of the West* (Boston: Houghton Mifflin, 1962), 2–4.

2. Kyle Hill, "Argumentum Ad Monsantum: Bill Maher and The Lure of a Liberal Logical Fallacy," *Scientific American Blog Network*, 2013, blogs.scientificamerican .com/but-not-simpler/argumentum-ad-monsantum-bill-maher-and-the-lure-of-a -liberal-logical-fallacy/.

3. Atifete Jahjaga, "Kosovar President Atifete Jahjaga: The Four Key Ingredients for Peace," The Hill, 2012. thehill.com/policy/international/232703-kosovar-president -atifete-jahjaga-the-four-key-ingredients-for-peace.

4. John Wesley Powell, *Report on the Land of the Arid Regions of the United Sates*, 2nd ed. (Washington, DC: Government Printing Office, 1879). hdl.handle.net/2027/ mdp.39015028143686.

5. Edward R. Murrow, "Wires and Lights in a Box: Speech before the Radio-Television News Directors Association," Radio Television Digital News Association,1958, www.rtdna.org/content/edward_r_murrow_s_1958_wires_lights _in_a_box_speech

6. Nate Silver, "'Signal' and 'Noise': Prediction as Art and Science," NPR *Fresh Air*, 2010. www.npr.org/2012/10/10/162594751/signal-and-noise-prediction-as-art-and -science.

7. Rich Karlgaard, "Internet Guru: Google Evangelist Vint Cerf," *Forbes*, May 2011, www.forbes.com/forbes/2011/0606/opinions-rich-karlgaard-innovation-rules -internet-guru.html.

8. Douglas Coupland, "The Interview: Douglas Coupland," *Maclean's*, September 2009, www.macleans.ca/culture/its-precipitating-a-real-philosophical-crisis-that-i -find-quite-fascinating/.

9. Emily Oster, "Take Back Your Pregnancy; Modern Pregnancy Comes with a Long List of Strict Rules, But Does It Have To? An Economist Examines the Data and Finds Room for Choice Amid the Familiar Limits," *Wall Street Journal*, August 9, 2013.

Index

About the Author

Donald A. Barclay has worked as a librarian since 1990, initially focusing on reference service and library instruction, but eventually branching into information technology and library administration. He has worked as a librarian at New Mexico State University (1990–1996), the University of Houston (1996–1997), and the Houston Academy of Medicine–Texas Medical Center Library (1997–2002). Since 2002 he has worked at the University of California, Merced, where he is currently the deputy university librarian. Prior to working as a librarian, he was an adjunct lecturer in English at Boise State University (1985–1990) as well as a US Forest Service firefighter (1976–1986). He holds a BA in English from Boise State University (1981), an MA in English from the University California, Berkeley (1985), and a master of library and information studies from the University of California, Berkeley (1990). He has published a number of books on library topics as well as books on the literature of the American West.

Barclay is a nationally recognized leader in the areas of evaluating information and teaching people to identify fake news. He published a widely read article, "The Challenge Facing Libraries in the Era of Fake News," in the *Conversation* (January 2017), was interviewed about fake news on the Matt Townsend radio program (February 2017), presented on "The Role of Librarians in an Era of Fake News, Alternative Facts, and Information

Overload" at the Coalition for Networked Information Meeting (April 2017), and was chosen by the American Library Association to lead a national webinar, "Fake News, Real Concerns: Developing Information Literate Students" (July 2017).